First World War
and Army of Occupation
War Diary
France, Belgium and Germany

58 DIVISION
Headquarters, Branches and Services
Royal Army Veterinary Corps
Deputy Assistant Director Veterinary Services
24 January 1917 - 31 January 1919

WO95/2994/6

The Naval & Military Press Ltd
www.nmarchive.com
Published in association with The National Archives

Published by

The Naval & Military Press Ltd

Unit 10 Ridgewood Industrial Park,

Uckfield, East Sussex,

TN22 5QE England

Tel: +44 (0) 1825 749494

www.naval-military-press.com

www.nmarchive.com

This diary has been reprinted in facsimile from the original. Any imperfections are inevitably reproduced and the quality may fall short of modern type and cartographic standards.

© Crown Copyright
Images reproduced by permission of The National Archives, London, England, 2015.

Contents

Document type	Place/Title	Date From	Date To
Heading	WO95/2994/6		
Heading	58th Division Asst Dir. Veterinary Services Jan 1917 Jan 1919		
War Diary	Southampton	24/01/1917	24/01/1917
War Diary	Havre	24/01/1917	26/01/1917
War Diary	Auxi Le Chateau	27/01/1917	27/01/1917
War Diary	Frohen Le Grand	02/02/1917	06/02/1917
War Diary	Lucheux	07/02/1917	20/02/1917
War Diary	Henu	24/02/1917	28/02/1917
War Diary	Bavincourt	01/03/1917	29/03/1917
War Diary	Lucheux	30/03/1917	01/04/1917
War Diary	Frohen Le Grand	02/04/1917	05/04/1917
War Diary	Bus Les Artois	06/04/1917	17/04/1917
War Diary	Achiet Le Grand	18/04/1917	22/04/1917
War Diary	Achiet Le Grand	19/04/1917	27/04/1917
War Diary	Bihucourt Camp	27/04/1917	27/04/1917
War Diary	Achiet Le Grand	30/04/1917	30/04/1917
War Diary	Bihucourt Camp	30/04/1917	02/05/1917
War Diary	Achiet Le Grand	02/05/1917	02/05/1917
War Diary	Bihucourt Camp	02/05/1917	05/05/1917
War Diary	Achiet Le Grand	05/05/1917	09/05/1917
War Diary	Bihucourt Camp	09/05/1917	09/05/1917
War Diary	Achiet Le Grand	09/05/1917	14/05/1917
War Diary	Bihucourt Camp	14/05/1917	17/05/1917
War Diary	Achiet Le Grand	13/05/1917	18/05/1917
War Diary	Bihucourt Camp	20/05/1917	23/05/1917
War Diary	Achiet Le Grand Camp	23/05/1917	23/05/1917
War Diary	Bihucourt Camp	23/05/1917	24/05/1917
War Diary	Achiet Le Grand	25/05/1917	25/05/1917
War Diary	Bihucourt Camp	25/05/1917	26/05/1917
War Diary	Achiet Le Grand	26/05/1917	26/05/1917
War Diary	Bihucourt Camp	26/05/1917	26/05/1917
Miscellaneous	H.Q 58th Divn	02/05/1917	02/05/1917
War Diary	Achiet Le Grand	27/05/1917	27/05/1917
War Diary	Bihucourt Camp	23/05/1917	29/05/1917
War Diary	Mory	30/05/1917	24/06/1917
War Diary	Courcelles	25/06/1917	08/07/1917
War Diary	Ytres	09/07/1917	31/07/1917
War Diary	Fosseux	01/08/1917	23/08/1917
War Diary	Ypres Area	24/08/1917	30/09/1917
War Diary	Zutkerque	01/10/1917	19/10/1917
War Diary	Poperinghe	20/10/1917	24/10/1917
War Diary	Ypres Area	25/10/1917	16/11/1917
War Diary	Proven	17/11/1917	25/11/1917
War Diary	Nielle	25/11/1917	07/12/1917
War Diary	Ypres Area	08/12/1917	31/12/1917
War Diary	Elverdinghe	01/01/1918	08/01/1918
War Diary	Couthove	09/01/1918	20/01/1918
War Diary	Corbie	21/01/1918	08/02/1918
War Diary	Dampccurt	09/02/1918	13/03/1918

War Diary	Quierzy	13/03/1918	22/03/1918
War Diary	Bretigny	23/03/1918	24/03/1918
War Diary	Camelin	25/03/1918	25/03/1918
War Diary	Nampcel	26/03/1918	27/03/1918
War Diary	Audignicourt	30/03/1918	01/04/1918
War Diary	Chevillecourt	02/04/1918	03/04/1918
War Diary	Cutry	04/04/1918	04/04/1918
War Diary	Villers Cotterets	05/04/1918	05/04/1918
War Diary	Saleux	06/04/1918	27/04/1918
War Diary	St Riquier	28/04/1918	06/05/1918
War Diary	Molliens-Au-Bois	07/05/1918	17/05/1918
War Diary	Contay	18/05/1918	02/06/1918
War Diary	Molliens-Au-Bois	03/06/1918	10/06/1918
War Diary	Cavillon	11/06/1918	20/06/1918
War Diary	Beaucourt	20/06/1918	03/08/1918
War Diary	Querrieu	04/08/1918	12/08/1918
War Diary	St Gratien	13/08/1918	23/08/1918
War Diary	Heilly	24/08/1918	27/08/1918
War Diary	Morlancourt Area	28/08/1918	06/09/1918
War Diary	Maurepas	07/09/1918	11/09/1918
War Diary	Nurlu Area	12/09/1918	24/09/1918
War Diary	Montauban	25/09/1918	25/09/1918
War Diary	Mingoval	26/09/1918	30/09/1918
War Diary	Sains En Gohelle	01/10/1918	13/10/1918
War Diary	Les Brebis	14/10/1918	18/10/1918
War Diary	Moncheaux	19/10/1918	19/10/1918
War Diary	Bersee	20/10/1918	22/10/1918
War Diary	Planard	23/10/1918	31/10/1918
War Diary	Mouchin Planard	01/11/1918	07/11/1918
War Diary	Bleharies	08/11/1918	11/11/1918
War Diary	Beloeil	12/11/1918	20/11/1918
War Diary	Peruwelz	21/11/1918	31/01/1919

WO 95/2994/6

58TH DIVISION

ASST DIR. VETERINARY SERVICES
JAN 1917 – JAN 1919

58TH DIVISION

WAR DIARY
INTELLIGENCE SUMMARY.
(Erase heading not required.)

Army Form C. 2118.

Instructions regarding War Diaries and Intelligence Summaries are contained in F.S. Regs., Part II. and the Staff Manual respectively. Title pages will be prepared in manuscript.

Place	Date	Hour	Summary of Events and Information	Remarks and references to Appendices
Southampton	24/1/17	6 PM	Embarked with H.Q. Staff 58 (London) Div. on transport "North Western Miller" for HAVRE	HAVRE 1/4/5
HAVRE	25/1/17	3 a.m.	Arrived & disembarked at 12 noon. Proceeded to Rest Camp.	
"	26/1/17		Entrained at HAVRE leaving at 3 P.M.	
AUX LE CHATEAU	27/1/17		Arrived 3 P.M. Proceeded to FREVENT.	
FREVENT LE GRAND	29/1/17		Proceeded by motor Car to H.Q. III Army & reported my arrival to DDVS from whom I received instructions regarding return to be rendered etc.	
"	30/1/17		Proceeded to H.Q. III Army & interviewed DDVS with regard to vaccination of Horses, Buns etc.	

Geo H Bowell Cap/V
for Major,
A.D.V.S.
58th (LONDON) DIVISION.

WAR DIARY
or
INTELLIGENCE SUMMARY
(Erase heading not required.)

Army Form C. 2118.

Instructions regarding War Diaries and Intelligence Summaries are contained in F.S. Regs., Part II. and the Staff Manual respectively. Title pages will be prepared in manuscript.

Place	Date	Hour	Summary of Events and Information	Remarks and references to Appendices
FROHEN LE GRAND	2/2/17		Forwarded roll of parc Micurs to Bacrs Ricards.— A.D.V.S. Major J. PEDDIE, 2i.c. M.V.S. Capt. N.K. TOMPSON, attached 290 Bgde R.F.A. Capt. J. SCOTT BOWDEN, attached 291 Bgde R.F.A. Capt. F.J. RICHMOND, attached 292 Bgde R.F.A. Capt. W.D. JORDAN, stating that Capt. R.A. STEWART attached Divisional Train A.S.C., & Capt. R.V.G. LAISTER attached D.A.C. had not yet arrived from England	
do	3/2/17		Issued detailed instructions to T.P.O's regarding procedure when animals are left behind by troops with influenza.	
do	4/2/17		Capt. Q.A. STEWART, A.S.C. reported his arrival from England with 5/2 Coy. A.S.C. Divisional H.Q. moved to LUCHEUX. Mobile Veterinary Section moved from FROHEN LE GRAND to GROUCHES.	
LUCHEUX	7/2/17		D.D.V.S. III army advised by telegram that Major J. PEDDIE, A.D.V.S. had been taken ill & removed to 37 Casualty Clearing Station. Capt. J. SCOTT BOWDEN ℞/o T.P. assumed duties as a/A.D.V.S. Visit from D.D.V.S. III Army who issued instructions for me (2/Lt. P. Bowden Capt.) to carry on the duties as acting A.D.V.S.	
LUCHEUX	8/2/17		Capt. R.V.G. LAISTER A.V.C. reported his arrival from England with 58 D.A.C.	

WAR DIARY
or
INTELLIGENCE SUMMARY.

Army Form C. 2118.

(Erase heading not required.)

Instructions regarding War Diaries and Intelligence Summaries are contained in F. S. Regs., Part II. and the Staff Manual respectively. Title pages will be prepared in manuscript.

Place	Date	Hour	Summary of Events and Information	Remarks and references to Appendices
LUCHEUX	10/2/17		Conference of all V.O's at H.Q. Reported to DDVS that Major J. PEDDIE was unfit probably he S.of R. got 10 days. Capt. M.K. TOMPSON S.o R. with quarters.	
do	11/2/17		Made special application to DDVS for provision of horse float.	
do	12/2/17		Instructions received from DDVS to mallein (intra dermo palpebral test) all horses of the division & include Nominal Roll of pre personnel attached to Artillery & Infantry Brigades showing days & hours of embarkation & disembarkation forwarded to O'l'c A+ & Remounts to DDVS To army	
do	13/2/17		Capt. M.D. JORDAN M.C. detailed to accompany the attached to 293rd Bgd. R.F.A, on the K.course of this unit to Army Field Artillery.	
do	14/2/17		DDVS TH Army advised that climatic conditions & shortage of rations test seriously affected bodily condition of animals in the Division. Advised DDVS Capt. Q.A. STEWART had met with serious accident this a.m. that Major J. PEDDIE had been evacuated to Base & of continued illness of Capt. M.K. TOMPSON. Also that on account of sickness of officers Mallein testing could not be undertaken at present. Veterinary Officers asked for to replace those evacuated q-d-s/?	
do	18/2/17			
do	19/2/17		Capt. M.K. TOMPSON evacuated to Hospital, M.O. & A.D.M.S. Consider him unfit for further service in the Field. J.W.	

Army Form C. 2118.

WAR DIARY
or
INTELLIGENCE SUMMARY.
(Erase heading not required.)

Instructions regarding War Diaries and Intelligence Summaries are contained in F. S. Regs., Part II. and the Staff Manual respectively. Title pages will be prepared in manuscript.

Place	Date	Hour	Summary of Events and Information	Remarks and references to Appendices
LUCHEUX.	23/2/17		Reported to DDVS III Army my anxiety for the health of the animals in the Division without further assistance. 50% of V.O.S sick & divisional units very scattered.	
HENU.	24/2/17		Moved with D.H.Q to HENU. Sgt P.C. ATTENBOROUGH A.V.C. attached to "D" Battery 293 Bgde. R.F.A. Temporarily posted to M.V.S on demobilization of his battery. Capt. M.K. TOMPSON %c M.V.S returned to duty.	
do	26/2/17		Mobile Veterinary Section moved from CROUCHES to HUMBERCAMP.	
do	27/2/17		Report sent to D.H.Q with reference to invaluable failing & poor condition of horses belonging to Div Train, Artillery & R.A.C. owing to bad condition of roads. M.T out of action, & double work thrown on to H.T. Capt. M.K. TOMPSON again reported sick (severe Rheumatism) Report to DDVS that the following Micros had reported for duty Capt. E. EVANS, A.V.C 26.2.17 & Capt. J.G. TAYLOR. 27.2.17 had been posted to Divisional Artillery.	
do	28/2/17		Mange Dipping Baths at LECROS TISON FARM allotted for use of Division March 1 to 9" inclusive. Made arrangements with V.O's unit commanders for use of same.	

J.W. Bowdler Capt.
Major A.D.V.S.
58th (LONDON) DIVISION.

WAR DIARY
INTELLIGENCE SUMMARY

Army Form C. 2118.

Place	Date	Hour	Summary of Events and Information	Remarks and references to Appendices
BAVINCOURT	1/3/17		Moved from HENU with D.H.Q. to BAVINCOURT.	
do	2/3/17		Conference of V.O's at this Office. Now posted as follows: Capt. F.T. RICHMOND O.C. not Rely. West. Capt. J.G. TAYLOR attached 290 Bgde R.F.A. Capt. E. EVANS att. 291 Bgde R.F.A. Capt. R.W. GLAISTER att. D.A.C. Capt. Q.A. STEWART still unfit for duty. Reported to D.H.Q. on unsatisfactory conditions at LA BAZIQUE (location of Div Train) for horses.	
do	3/3/17		Inspection by D.D.V.S. III Army of Batteries of 150 A.F.A. Bgde (attached for Rely Service) 33 horses evacuated to Base for Mange.	
do	4/3/17		Inspection by D.D.V.S III Army of Ammunition Column of 150 A.F.A. Bgde and 115 A.F.A. Bgde. Ammunition Column at LA BAZIQUE FARM. Report to D.H.Q with reference to unsatisfactory rationing arrangements at BAILLEUVAL.	
do	9/3/17		Conference of V.O's at this Office. Present:- 58 Div V.O's:- Capt. RICHMOND, GLAISTER, EVANS, & TAYLOR. Attached Officers:- Capt. M.D. JORDAN (293 A.F.A Bgde). Capt. R. MOOSE (150 A.F.A. Bgde) & Capt. A.K. MEEKE (115 A.F.A Bgde).	
do	10/3/17		Advice received from D.V.S. through D.D.V.S. III Army to instruct Capt. M.K. TOMSON to report for duty to N°8. Rely Hospital. FORGES LES EAUX.	
do	11/3/17		Sergt. M.L. CROUCHER A.V.C. att. 173 Inf. Bgde met with accident & admitted to Field Ambulance.	

WAR DIARY or INTELLIGENCE SUMMARY

Army Form C. 2118.

Place	Date	Hour	Summary of Events and Information	Remarks and references to Appendices
BAVINCOURT	11.3.17		Cont'd. Lieut. P.C. ATTENBOROUGH A.V.C. temporarily attached to 173 Infy. Byde. Reports accordingly to DDVS III Army. Submitted affiliation through D.H.Q. on A.F. W.3342. M.S. 3522/1 for temporary promotion in accordance with two histories regarding promotion of officers. Sect. III Para. 1(d)	
do	12/3/17		Report to DDVS that Capt. Q.A. STEWART A.V.C. had been admitted to 43 C.C.S. for evacuation to Base suffering from a fractured foot. Officer to replace him required till.	
do	13/3/17		Reported to D.H.Q. & D.V.S. that a total of 1955 animals had been dipped at the mange dipping baths, during the period it was allotted to the Division. Reported Capt. W.R. TOWNSON's departure to FORBES.LES.EAUX.	
do	14/3/17		Submitted report of preference with regards to periods of years most suitable for clipping horses & its connection with regard to mange outbreaks. Conferred by DDVS Conference of V.O.s at BAVINCOURT re demonstration by Capt. WILLIAMSON A.V.C. who demonstrated Mallein Testing. Report to D.V.S. that Capt. Q.A. STEWART had been evacuated to Base 14.3.17. Received telegram from D.V.S. 1st Army that Major H. CREENFIELD A.V.C. had been directed to proceed to 58 Div. as ADVS.	
do	17/3/17		Forwarded further report to D.H.Q. & DDVS stating animals of Div. are still loosing	JGS.

WAR DIARY
or
INTELLIGENCE SUMMARY.

Army Form C. 2118.

Place	Date	Hour	Summary of Events and Information	Remarks and references to Appendices
BAYINCOURT	17/3/17		Cont. condition especially A.S.C. artillery & D.A.C. stabling ability & exhaustion caused through overwork, armistice ground, softness & short rations an chief cause	
do	18/3/17		Major H. GREENFIELD. A.V.C reported for duty as A.D.V.S.	

W.M. Bowden Capt.
a/ A.D.V.S.
58th (LONDON) DIVISION.

Army Form C. 2118.

ADVS. 58th Division

MAJOR H GREENFIELD
MC

WAR DIARY
or
INTELLIGENCE SUMMARY.
(Erase heading not required.)

Instructions regarding War Diaries and Intelligence Summaries are contained in F. S. Regs., Part II. and the Staff Manual respectively. Title pages will be prepared in manuscript.

Place	Date	Hour	Summary of Events and Information	Remarks and references to Appendices
BAVINCOURT	18/3/17		Arrived on appointment ADVS. 58th Div. Reported arrival DDVS DVS III Army. Supervision of VOs as follows. Capt J. Scott BOWDEN acting ADVS i/c 1/10 North. Sn Divn. F.Amb. (Lumn Amb. 26 Rumanian) Capt F J RICHMOND 58 MOB VETY SECT. Capt J E TAYLOR 290 Bde RFA 173 Bde Pioneer group. Capt. E. Evans. 291 Bry RFA 174th Pioneer Group. Capt R W GLAISTER 58th Sqd. 175 Sp Piny groups attached. Capt WD JORDAN 293 Bny RFA 90 Dy Piny. Mobile Field Amb. SIALCOT PIONEERS — in 3rd Indian Bnt. Capt RWOOFF 150 AFA. I.A.C. Capt AV MEECE 168th AFA 84 I.A.C. 2/3 Indian Piny. New gun teams	
"	19/3/17		Inspect at LA CAUCHIE. ~ C Battery 290 Bny. in open barn, horses poor + emaciated, (mgs. worn pgs.) 3 Field Ambulances. Horse teams troopers forage stable. 2/2 H.C. Field Amb. Horses + equip't good. 2/1 Field Amb; hrd - animals poor rugs + noskings out of repair or deficient. Horse no cover — 3 supply only — OC notified 2/3 H.C. Field Amb. horses poor not rugged (see letter HUMBER CAMPS) HQ. 290 Bny RFA. 36 horses. good. BSM to their horses from PAS. Generally very bad. no rugs blankets nothing a Bye recommend the bad horses 290 Bny be centralized under cover at LA CAUCHIE. Start to Inspect 2/3 R. Jackie Bdr Transport at near HUMBER CAMPS turn out - animals good. Visit 58 MOBILE VETY SECT - officer away a duty. Senior NCO sick, men absent, attached men not working. Situation bad. Cold, wet + note supply bad. billets - kitchens very dirty.	

WAR DIARY or INTELLIGENCE SUMMARY

Army Form C. 2118.

A.D.V.S. 58th Div'n

Place	Date	Hour	Summary of Events and Information	Remarks and references to Appendices
BAVINCOURT	20/3/17		Weather very wet. Roads & standings bad.	
			Inspected 174 Inf Bde Transport BAILLEULMONT. Trans scale insufficient. Known - N.C.O.s inspecting.	
			Inoculating 2/6 London Regt.	
			S.B.R.O. Rifles horses at work. Arrangement & management poor. Synopsis complete.	
			2/7 London Regt. horses Synopsis good.	
			2/5 London Regt. horses very good & well done. (mag horseshoe inspect 50%)	
			Inspected 291 Bde R.F.A (with C.R.A.) Farriers special report Synops. 2 DAs II wrong	
			A Batt. 40 unsound below standard 36 unsound below standard	
			B " 25 horses below standard 22 " " 2 " unsuitable any horse ?		1 shot at 291 [Synops?]
			C " 26 " 25 "	Low in condition	immoveable
			D " 19 " 10 "		
			Horses rapidly losing condition well cared for.	
			Horses rapidly losing condition in hos from short days, arrange for 70 feeds, mounts for 3 hour to hrs. BAILLEULMONT. A.D. i C Battery, half the horses do nop. Extra meetings on hyped.	
			Report on moving this Brigade to provided mats 150 Command anthrax - dalang Synops	
			Horses be completed at once, and animal to protected in hutting in shelters as	
			area - without which of exposure Synops will decrease immensely in short period of	
			protected conditions.	
			Inst. CRA Inspect horses A Bde & 290 Bde R.F.A. horses & synops complete & good generally in [illegible]	

Army Form C. 2118.

WAR DIARY
or
INTELLIGENCE SUMMARY.
(Erase heading not required.)

ADvS 58th Division

Place	Date	Hour	Summary of Events and Information	Remarks and references to Appendices
BAVINCOURT	29/3/17		Standings open holt and very expired	the
"	30/3/17		DDvS III army inspected horses 24/1st Bay RCA. BAILLEUVAL, BASSEUX the changes as follows	
			A Battery. 14 for evacuation 5 may poor remainder poor	
			B " 27 " " 8 " " poor	
			C " 34 " " 11 " " poor	
			D " 20 " " 6 " " fair	
			ATA Brigade taken from the Division and ADS of Division 4 (HEATH) to IDATA 5E 293A/A	the
			duty retired - It is noted to them that horses both at GRAND TRSON is available	
			and required for their units will data prepared for such	
	31/3/17		Evacuated 111 horses sick to BASE. 1 horse drowned	
			Inspected 240 Bay RCA. C Battery, 1 horses → poor quality condition mgs/3 short markings 5D	
			recommend 15 for evacuation. 31 unfit for duty, under shelter stalls at LA CAUCHIE.	the
			B Battery 6 below strength 26 horses at LA CAUCHIE (remainder battery position) recommend	
			11 for evacuation 13 unfit for duty no mgs available 6 markings to Depot to Depot required.	
			at BERLES. D Battery. 16 horses under strength recommend 23 for evacuation 24 unfit for duty	
			remainder poor. All horses under shelter Egypt. very deficient	the

T2134. Wt. W708—776. 500000. 4/15. Sir J. C. & S.

Army Form C. 2118.

WAR DIARY
or
INTELLIGENCE SUMMARY.
(Erase heading not required.)

ASVS 58th Divn

Place	Date	Hour	Summary of Events and Information	Remarks and references to Appendices
BAVINCOURT	27/3/17		Inspected 2/10 Lond. Regt (175 Inf Bde) marching into BERLES & horse lines my part. Horses & Equipt generally good.	
			LA BEDIQUE FARM. 512 Co Div Train. Stabling water arrangement & Equipt good. Wagon lines and approach very bad (requires 3/pr heavy draught horses to pull an empty GS wagon) 12 pair horses not in work in good condition. Equipt good	
			509 Co A.S.C Div Train. 65 horses not at work very good. 50 horses rept deficient order N.O.s - proceed with general tests with mealies of all horses in Division whom not in work or on sick horse lines.	Nil
"	28/3/17		Conference of V.O.s at D H Q. They report the completion of 1000 million tests. They are impressed with the necessity of earlier recognition of weak horses (dead rate too high) The care of horses in Division to improve. Stables must be empty & intelligent more. Horse Exercise rugs washing & butter chaff for (in Infantry Dept 30 m.p h.m at an morning meal) DDVS orders transmitted that full protection examination are to be done in every horse from Salonika; lice cases to be treated with oil of vaseline; enquiries to same by V.O.s inspected too thoroughly are too frequent.	
			V.O.s are notified they must inform A.SgT at once of unstrum of for horses are too severe, horses in trench, bad state of harness &c, in immediate town supplied seriously from reinforcements in Division, horses of ambulances too horses in remount.	Nil

Army Form C. 2118.

(12)

Assts 58th RE

WAR DIARY
or
INTELLIGENCE SUMMARY.
(Erase heading not required.)

Instructions regarding War Diaries and Intelligence Summaries are contained in F. S. Regs., Part II. and the Staff Manual respectively. Title pages will be prepared in manuscript.

Place	Date	Hour	Summary of Events and Information	Remarks and references to Appendices
BAVINCOURT	24/3/17		ADVS III army inspected 58 mounted WRC Akela took PAS. A small part on the Roads very bad indeed in this area. G. was impossible for two days MARLINCOURT BIENVILLERS. Inspected A Sub/div OC. 181 mules 85 horses 8 pairs harnesses good. arrangement, Egypt Corn 9 animals good. 5th CATC Sub/div strength 58, for inoculation ?, poor mops for Arty 11. Sect 9. Remounts 98 prev. horses to BMS. Obtain MT ought for new convoys to BMS from PA, as not very clear what mules to renew HPs quickly enough from incoming time weekly to BMS.	
	25/3/17		Weekly state 9 took 1 horse for BMS in future. Remaining was transmitted 25/3 Total 507. Found 18 v unimproved 164. Died 42 Destroyed 13 missing 0 Running 150 Total 507. Strength 3678 horses mules got total 15900ish. Depot STS 7 & RS BIENVILLERS in accordance with urgent instructions DOS report. Translation (H other bodies) all farm & mops for horses Egypt generally good. Obtain mules transport relay for this coy/coy to mount harnesses. Improve 50th Fill & PAS POMMIER 1 cow for inoculation & other mops for chsty. Equipt my deficient small rephobal report to CRE Remorque removed from Achiet la Petit BMP. Signed to have ford not receipts 2 from in letter.	N/a

T2134. Wt. W708-776. 500000. 4/15. Sir J. C. & S.

Army Form C. 2118.

WAR DIARY
or
INTELLIGENCE SUMMARY.
(Erase heading not required.)

Instructions regarding War Diaries and Intelligence Summaries are contained in F. S. Regs., Part II. and the Staff Manual respectively. Title pages will be prepared in manuscript.

AD&OS 58th Division

Place	Date	Hour	Summary of Events and Information	Remarks and references to Appendices
BAPINCOURT	20/3/17		Weather again very wet & cold, roads in bad condition. Inspected horses ADINFER — water troughs reported & pumps to fill them; hut[?] & HPO supply appears good for present but troughs pumps & programme of times for work fully reported on; much economy of water place made. 510 Co MTC St L. Amm. Strength 50. 3 omnibus B+D check — attached 7 no. 16 numbers SGS 0 AEC. 5 inspt for duty remainder in poor condition, work hand[?] moderate. Horses appear to turn respond recently working from LA BEZIQUE & Take onwards BELLEVUE 5 Sr Lce L.R. and in poor block roads and in long deviation for milking. (20-25 mile) 291st/Bty RFA. C Battery standings approved. rest. recommended more sheltered position. no further turn of condition, 3 evacuated since inspection 24/3/17 1 sick. B Battery. no change of condition, standings good. 2 " 7 D " no change of condition, standings open & wet H.J. Sick ones in present 27/3/17. The horses of this Brigade were not in such slightly work, roads twenty several. They had previously enjoyed most pure experience at PAS and are not in full work owing 20 mile a day. At Bucy & MAGNI. A Battery 291 Bty RFA. Good standings for horses being made. Few shelter for men. Horses look in more condition. 7 evacuated 1 died 1 destroyed. Remounts apt.	

Army Form C. 2118.

A.D.V.S. 58th Divn

WAR DIARY
or
INTELLIGENCE SUMMARY.
(Erase heading not required.)

Place	Date	Hour	Summary of Events and Information	Remarks and references to Appendices
BAVINCOURT	26/3/17		Inspected horses 13. 290 R.F.A. 101 horses present. 4 evacuated to 4th remount by ambulance horse. Horses generally in good condition. No rugs available but suitable blankets in use.	
"	27/3/17		Inspected 21 London Regt (173 Inf Bng) at LA HERLIÈRE. Horses + Transport well cared for good. C Batty 290 Brig R.F.A. LA CAUCHIE. 4/fr inspection 14 mspt for duty. 3 destroyed. Such since last inspection 22/3/17. Much improvement in animals condition which are not + harden. Comm. Report to 579TD + CRA more care of horses required. B Batty 290 R.F.A. 4 Horses inspected. A " " " farm horses inspected cond in. Report to 579TD + CRA. BERLES. Standing lost + reported over 12 horses. Hut condition Horses commented upon + condition. In reply to VII Corps + report horses evacuated low in condition + urgently requiring fresh intake. C & 6 dead 11.95. A 6×12. 300 + 290 R.f.A. 340 Sgn. "CRA 140 DAC. 730 Division tc.	

H Greenfield
Major,
A.D.V.S.
58th (LONDON) DIVISION.

A.D.M.S.
27/3/17

Army Form C. 2118.

WAR DIARY
or
INTELLIGENCE SUMMARY.
(Erase heading not required.)

A.D.V.S. 58th Division
MAJOR H GREENFIELD

Instructions regarding War Diaries and Intelligence Summaries are contained in F. S. Regs., Part II. and the Staff Manual respectively. Title pages will be prepared in manuscript.

Place	Date	Hour	Summary of Events and Information	Remarks and references to Appendices
BARLY COURT	28/3/17		Recommendations for water troughs, forage protection against spread of glanders. Sulheris by enemy agents as reported —	HG
			Arrange completion of mallein test of 3rd & 2nd Divn. V.O.'s L. work in Lines as high rate with approved COs.	
	29/3/17		R A units with V.O's attached transferred to 21st Division. A.D.V.S. notified 3 Divn, and 28 Land Regt bsgr BIENVILLERS, A.D.V.S. 21st Divn at TRAIN LA BEZIQUE, 4 Land Regt DAINVILLE.	
			D.H.Q. move to LUCHEUX 174 Bde Pay Group to LUCHEUX 175 HALLOY MORIVETY SECT & MONDICOURT	
	29/3/17 30/3/17		Weather very wet — had rough very bad. Can get no communication with V.O. 291 Bry 1 R.F.A.	HG
			Inspect D.A.C. WARLINCOURT H.Q.; condition of animals generally good; equipt gent ammunition LA BEZIQUE to ADINFER and back. Unit surrounded by 24 mile journey with ammunition B ECHELON to horses for inoculation, 16 down unfit for duty mohine & very lame — remainder generally in fair condition — British mules took from 504 Co R.E. - 3rd LABOUR Batt much debilitated from overwork, irregular feeding — Animals in good shelter & approx well cared for.	HG
			Heavy rains — roads very bad.	
LUCHEUX	30.3.17		Inspect 511 F.C. R.E. animals (infant) appear well cared for. Equipt good & in excellent condition. Can get no communication with V.O. 291 Bry 1 R.F.A.	
	31.3.17		Inspect animals 2/1 F.Amb. at MONDICOURT. They show some improvement. (for inoculation & inspect for Sy/s.) (detail in report).	HG

Army Form C. 2118.

WAR DIARY
or
INTELLIGENCE SUMMARY.
(Erase heading not required.)

Army Troops. 58th Division

Place	Date	Hour	Summary of Events and Information	Remarks and references to Appendices
LUCHEUX	31.3.17		Arrange for vaccination of some sick animals, hot HP. Det and more of wounded not during. Inspect transport to Ind. Regt. GREVAS (11 short 12 on details WALLEY) condition fair, shoes again of same amount. Transport good. The horses 173 Dp Pony HP are in excellent condition at PROMERA - there 2/3 Lond. Regt. mules in open field - good - horses upon one 20 y. old has b/l laceration of bryskit defrient regimen completion. At Inspection horses (19 shod) 508 F. Co R.E. HALLOY - horses been standing in heavy rain & deep mud, some without clothing, mostly empty not removed & one newly moving about, some horses hypoth in mud - he cows found in village which in regard regimend and available for a number of animals. Report E. I Staff 174 Dp Pony march out without transport, grazped, making is impossible for TOs to control - Some rode out fell when manoeuvre for hay held road, others not "seen" feet as "ashy" paint.	H.R.
"	1.4.17		DH.Q. march to FROHEN AU GRAND. MOB. VETY SECT. to b stop night at GROUCHES, middle ground roads very heavy, hilly, weather wet. 174 Dp Pong. Group at BOUQUEMAIS. 195 Dp B & MEURLETTE Hq. next MOB. VETY SECT. near FROHEN-LE-GRAND Transport 174 Dp Pony much worn in from of injuring.	H.R.
FROHEN LE GRAND	2.4.17		FONTAINE - D'ETALON area. 195 Inf Pony Gp. here fallen in to MOEUX.	

T2134. Wt. W708-776. 500000. 4/15. Sir J. C. & S.

Army Form C. 2118.

WAR DIARY
or
INTELLIGENCE SUMMARY.
(Erase heading not required.)

ADVS 58th DIV

Place	Date	Hour	Summary of Events and Information	Remarks and references to Appendices
FROHEN LE GRAND	2/4/17		Dropped transport on march. Finding when SOS 7.G. 85 not trained to brought new remounts required for emergency, remounts SOS Field & B.S. marching tired 11.30 P.M. without first watering for day. Feeding system not satisfactory.	HR
"	3/4/17		Division is to move to hut yet not anticipated entrain to DHQ for information re their condition on account of horses in remounts due to heavy work & weather. Say should be given in large sizes. 173 Inf Brig Group. march (men in trees, transport light) to BOIS DE MAISON for duty VII Corps. 5 horses evacuated through No. 73 VETY SECT. Transport control guard. Weekly state. (delayed by 291 Bdy RGA not yet communicating, without which DDVS report does not (return) as follows. Remounting 150 admitted 24 ev Total 41st unsound 3-5 ?unrepair? 1.A.C. Died 3(?) distroyed 2.3. Remaining 140 Total +26. Strength horses 2789 mules 1054 Total 3?47? 3771 Rs. Orders revived 10.30 P.M. 174 Inf Brig to march 20-22 miles 4/4/17 65-16 miles 5/4/17	HR
FROHEN LE GRAND			Forward inspection reports 174 Inf Brig, 173 Inf Brig, 1CE unit FOSTHQ. and submit memorandum for circular re improvement in care of horses, as there is great disparity in care and condition of mounts. Journey mum can be done in some units.	JB
FROHEN LE GRAND	4/4/17		Wire and submit report to DDVS that owing to condition of roads & remounts is is impossible 174 Inf Brig can complete march today and impossible for them to reach destination tomorrow; that the casualties & wastage will be high. Explanation added why condition of remounts is such- mainly horses shipped out in JANUARY arrived FRANCE on unmounted depot into worst weather; loss appears in ?pher?, & detailed return re the above same on hand tomorrow. Work condition in 7th in 7th INF	HR

T134. Wt. W708—776. 500000. 4/15. Sir J. C. & S.

Army Form C. 2118.

Instructions regarding War Diaries and Intelligence Summaries are contained in F.S. Regs., Part II. and the Staff Manual respectively. Title pages will be prepared in manuscript.

WAR DIARY
or
INTELLIGENCE SUMMARY.
(Erase heading not required.)

ANZAC 5th Div.

Place	Date	Hour	Summary of Events and Information	Remarks and references to Appendices
FROHEN LE GRAND	4/4/17		and MARCH was dreadful, and which movement had been continuous is highlighted by shortage of transport including dumping of rifles & equipt — and animals have been much improved & weather & new Standings.	
			Evacuate a cat. horses from DOULLENS.	
			174th Inf. Bgd. (Capt SCOTT BOWDEN AVC joining on T.O.) marches 20-22 miles CHERIENNE — FONTAINE L'ETALON to AUTHEUVLE & AMPLIER — mass & Bus.— Transport as purble & road— Some roads Australian remounts spread moving 10 mile track in January to NAVANS. 3 animals destroyed. 20 shelled on collected by MoB. VETY SECT.	
			Report to STHQ 174th Inf. Bgd. Transport marches in a different & not separate groups with no staff officers, staying for 5 hours through FROHEN-LE-GRAND — and the first & last 2 mile fatigue was given to come amid before the commencement, the arrangements for stragglers was improved by STHQ HQ.	
"	5/4/17		MoB. VETY SECT movements goes harder with 175 Inf Bgd Group to AMPLIER.	
			AHQ move to E. Bus.-les-ARTOIS.	
			Movement 174 Inf Bgd group columns towards MAILLY MALLET which is reached by most right Transport tail of column reaches AMPLIER and operates through AUTHIE & Bus.les.ARTOIS; animals	
			2/1 and 2/2 7Anls reach 511 Co ASC much exhausted. At end of March 174 Bgd + 1 horse dead, 7 more evacuated Vty. wasted had roads very bad to HEM. 2nd DOULLENS area from Bus les ARTOIS to M.Vgtrre.	

WAR DIARY
or
INTELLIGENCE SUMMARY.
(Erase heading not required.)

Army Form C. 2118.

ADVS 37th Divn

Place	Date	Hour	Summary of Events and Information	Remarks and references to Appendices
BUS-LES ARTOIS	6/4/17		Report arrival to DDVS. VII Army & information that was attached to 31st Division (later Capt Evans reported sick in hospital) 173 Bde (Bry until VII Corps hve arrived and unknown to write much afield, ask for their rly attendance thro' III Army, and ask for rail heads for evacuation of sick horses. Reply to DHQ. in Lorries of horses in rail to ABBEVILLE. Over 111 horses have been evac. since 1st, which other evacuation was ordered by DDVS III Army - every arrangement possible was made for their two rail journey evacuated many strays — and 2 railway accidents at ABBEVILLE killed a number and injured others - previous to receive there was only 1 horse drawn van truck. Submit to DHQ. that many F. condition y animals (Mounted Extraction, limber loads q) ammunition to reduced from 22 to 16 horses, and work to not attended to collect by animal transport.	He
BUS-LES ARTOIS	7/4/17		Sympts of dogs being distemper owing to recent weather, MOs very busy again at BUS. DDVS hosts office weather continues showery - roads never somewhat - Inspect horses of 7 Amb - were work at BERTRAN COURT, SILAC working generally good 2nd W Signal Co lost much in condition. 2/3 Field Ambulance, horses, harness care & supply "good. Inspect 173rd Bde Bry transport. Generally in good working condition. 2/4 Lond. Brit. Strength 54 good, 1/1 Lond Bt good, 13/ 7 good, 3 short, a large number	He

Army Form C. 2118.

WAR DIARY
or
INTELLIGENCE SUMMARY.

(Erase heading not required.)

Army Troops 37th Divn

Place	Date	Hour	Summary of Events and Information	Remarks and references to Appendices
BVS-Les ARDIS	7/4/17		9 more casualties Syphilis disposed. T.O. appears to require more consideration re tents; 2/10 Lond Bath Cond good. Strength 56	
			The animals 503 7 & RE appears weak for march 13 miles, tomorrow arrange for some 5 draught horses from Mot Pay Sect., and submit their necessity for more E.D.A.Q.	
			174 Fwd Pony (two 1 Lon's MALLY MALLET) made ACHIET-le-GRAND.	K.
"	8/4/17		Weekly state submitted as follows. Remaining 170 Admitted 58 Total 228 Carried 62 Evacuated 54 Died 4 Destroyed 6 Remaining 96 Total 228 Strength Loss 9/10 Mules 2bo Total 1190.	
			Inspect. at MAILLY MALLET, sick animals II Army Aux Horse Co. arrange for vet to removed to ambulance. Transport 27 Lond Regt. (8 horses) animals in good working condition, one horse from 9 198 h.Gm Co. Dentr Returning from heavy fatigue Work will make marching t ACHIET le GRAND. 3 very lame t h one E hock W/st Sect. 2/4 h. Gm Co mules working well but neekup. ordered t stop yesperal that steen small attacks animals may be retained for TO's approvision. Weather good work's today	
			Heavy rain at night – snow in morning.	
"	9/4/17		Inspos Altitude 176 animals 51 BMC animals worn but last night – animals worn but in good working /th	

T2134. Wt. W708—776. 500000. 4/15. Sir J. C. & S.

WAR DIARY or INTELLIGENCE SUMMARY

Army Form C. 2118.

ARTOIS 57th Div

Place	Date	Hour	Summary of Events and Information	Remarks and references to Appendices
Bus-Les ARTOIS	9/4/17		Condition. Recent hard severe – portion from BIENVILLERS own lay had roads – weapons left under frost for night. 1 route thick in J[ourney]. 1 cyclist arrived from echelons. Submit report to 57th Div III Army (two sides I) suggest on a menage ccaro evacuated by Siff at 9 to 10 Dec in model completed. 9 from 57th Div 59 other ranks. Evidence support the view that shipping and shipping stops opened on menage. Evidence however, that shipping all one in route as close to home 57th Div transtures as horses from exhaustion very high and animals apparently improved... from wearing to exposure, exhaustion when grass grows work 1/3. Support of mountain mean shipping on action service to intimate & too high - in extra parts or rather which prohibits diagrams but does not render animal unacceptable. Experiments	
"	10/4/17		Capt EVARJS A/C 241st Bny RFA reported to be invalided out to BASE – Strong wm shower. Inspect with ACHIET-LC-GRAND – generally the repair solution from arm -- would be turned in the open which cannot be arranged by tying up horses to engines with end corners over the whole to windows & wide – 503 F.Co grant loss 9 day from strain of Kayaks	
"	11/4/17		7th Lanc Regt: Epyapt maryrits horses improved. horses 2/8 hard Regt well cared for 9 good 15-hand Regt Horses good. 5/11 Fo. RE Egypt. ment more more trace, from want of experience. Some falling off in condition of these animals. Farm horse tying worked on fatigues.	

WAR DIARY
or
INTELLIGENCE SUMMARY

Army Form C. 2118.

AROS S&M Division

Place	Date	Hour	Summary of Events and Information	Remarks and references to Appendices
BUS. ten AFFOIS	11/4/17		511 C.M.C. Horses being well done, condition improved. N.C.O. Stretchers. Great improvement in care of animals and their condition advanced accordingly. Some transport N.C.O. still insufficient in instruction or mounted recommended. Recommend corporal for promotion on 3 horses. 512 C.M.C. great improvement at MCHISI & PETIT well cared for and improving. Regret that of 3 pairs on detachment and 39 head Coys 3 dead & 1 dying. Report E.S.H.O. will not take their has two good riflemen of attached troops in return much of the horsemen coming seems wantage. Above remarks tempted to notice of much improved. Wants: roads not but teller generally ordered though rough for transport.	
"	12/4/17		Detail E.S.H.O. for Trinomazoan that dry Bullocks to guns lead horses for two horses to carry lore on animals. Thicks a risk – from scout's team on zilla. Took road B. Kudo especially ammunition have increased, condition of animals is low, few mules have spare animals and many on lilac strength. Relies could keep road around a great deal until help of the troops. Report: not 19 best. Some improvements but animals too much overloaded, treatment not sent transport of complete enough. Men work hard. No fresh of saddlery in Egypt. Records require improvement. this section has been much neglected of late.	No

WAR DIARY
or
INTELLIGENCE SUMMARY.

Army Form C. 2118.
(23)

ARTOIS. 5th MONTH

Place	Date	Hour	Summary of Events and Information	Remarks and references to Appendices
Bus les ARTOIS	13/4/17		R.A. unit returned to Division. 173 Inf. Bgy returned to Division at Bus les ARTOIS after severe work. Division some went in détachement. 4th Bde now at BOIRY known beyond F. cannot transmit with the Batt. held or no ley. H.Batts have done over 50 miles in 3 days. The horses unworked 16 hrs one day - pull limbers with rest exhausted animals over of bad roads. Horses of 58th Division on full forage ration. Capt REIDY AVC arrives for duty with 241st Bty/CFA.	
"	14/4/17	11.15	Animals of 7 Bde BERTRAN COURT neglected - Admin O. went. All S.O.'s dumped "should be warned that too work them more F & Shound. Inspect animals 43/67 Inf Bde. ACHEUX a good falling off in condition apparent from ACHEUX forage. 2 annuals for examination 6 others unfit for duty - Report accordingly. ADSD + Bde to examine g better report fit hors. That motor lorries with ambulance which is being now in account g horses lorries for sc reexam today. M. inspect 4/4 Innd Regt. 2 emaciated animals for examination. 1 & h/h.5 two private animals very fair - & month conduct by military of duty horsemen - required to wait for improvement -13 Lond Regt. No change in emaciated horses, sword out that two for 7 mth mapping are sounced to be examined for emergency shoes Appendices	14/h.
14/h.

WAR DIARY
or
INTELLIGENCE SUMMARY.

Army Form C. 2118.

Army. Sept Bearers

Place	Date	Hour	Summary of Events and Information	Remarks and references to Appendices
BUS LES ARTOIS	15/4/17		2/1st and 1/2 Lond Regt marching out (with 173, 13th ACHIET L'GRAND) turn sick by A.D. Inspect sick animals. Nost Hyg Sect. Considerable improvement. 7 for treatment. Weekly state Sept Bers. attacked as follows - Remaining 96 Admitted 131 Total 227 Evac'd 40 Transferred incl. died 8 destroyed 9 Remaining 17.3 Total 227 Strength horses 241 Mules 576 Total 1807. Circular letter EVDS - Copy of instruction 373. DDV2 Army for return; health Lee common. animals must be sent from work earlier, detail names men employed. Cases for death, weekly state required of wastage for each unit to approach causes of failure on cases of animals, arrangements must be made to transport sick mules to nearest V mobile in FRANCE.	Sept Brs
"	16/4/17		Arrange that Vety Sect. to remain at station for collection and evacuation of sick animals in district & for O.C. to inform boss 2/3 Field Ambulance ACHEUX Army Lost birth, left on detachment. Weather wet roads bad.	LANCASHIRE Dump BERTRANCOURT & AVALUY Sept Brs.
"	17.4.17		DHQ. moves to ACHIET LE GRAND. Weather army heavy rain. Roads roads improved but rough after heavy metalling.	Sept Brs
ACHIET LE GRAND	18/4/17		Visit 17 & 19 Coy Corps unit in district. Not V.O.F. Bn? Main. Arrange accn. & c for Mot Hyg Sect. with Camp Commandant I Corps	Sept Brs

WAR DIARY
or
INTELLIGENCE SUMMARY.

Army Form C. 2118.

(25)

A.D.M.S. 57th Division.

Place	Date	Hour	Summary of Events and Information	Remarks and references to Appendices
ACHIET-le-GRAND	19 26/4/17	a.m.	With C.R.A. inspect animals 58 D.A.C. 290 Bry. R.F.A. I am very sorry I could not find time to run for my Brit. transport or my recommendation	Ito.
"	28/4/17		with CRA inspect animals 291st Bry R.F.A. D.A.A. section D.A.C. Submit report on R.A. horses & D.H.Q. (Copy to D.D.V.S. I Army) a report on R.A. horses on arrival from duty, attachment to 2nd Division. Strength 611 short, 62 for concentration 108 others unfit for duty. Condition of remainder as follows:- 290 Bry R.F.A. A Battery 7 Good B- Poor C Fair D 7 Good H.Q. Poor 291 " A " B Good C 7 Good D Fair H.Q. Poor D.A.C. No 1 Sect. Good has Good h.3. V Poor There has been huge wastage in the past 14 days as follows 290 Bry 187, 291 Bry 124, DAC 97. This appears due to excessive work + exposure to severe weather, but also a large measure to want of sympy'S - So batteries are practically without a rug or blanket, nestling or tripod for a single horse. Its remainder dispersed of 75?. I recommend that horses A.D.A. and B Echelon D.A.C. be sent down from draught work & animals D.A.A. Sect. D.A.C. to returned to their unit for aggregation. Experience will continued night work and rest for batteries would help. The drawing of Batteries for much redmounted +	Ito.

Army Form C. 2118.

ADVS 5th Div 2B

WAR DIARY
or
INTELLIGENCE SUMMARY.
(Erase heading not required.)

Instructions regarding War Diaries and Intelligence Summaries are contained in F.S. Regs., Part II. and the Staff Manual respectively. Title pages will be prepared in manuscript.

Place	Date	Hour	Summary of Events and Information	Remarks and references to Appendices
ACHIET LE GRAND	20/4/17		effective work on horses indirectly through the men as well as by reserved ammunition cartage. H. Land. host. kept situation approx ACHIET LE GRAND.	
"	21/4/17		DDVS 5 Army inspected RA horses 5th Division, the condition of horses commented Generally, that their improvement continues to do but improvement will be impossible without good weather and rest; that the numbers arranged for evacuation are low but as strength of horses also low it is not possible to send many to what arrivals be desirable, owing to the military situation. Arrangements for special feeding RA horses - boiled feeds, frequent feeding, chaff, grazing generally good. Special NWD application being made for their clothing - Egypt. Two Batteries from XXVI Brigade RFA withdrawn from action for rest of personnel & horses, the remainder to follow after their return. Weekly state of sick lame submitted as follows - Remaining 158 Admitted 200 Total 358. Cured 88 Transferred 188 Died 94 Destroyed 42 Missing 9 Remaining 146 Strength 3487. Mules 1015 Total 3269.	Nil Nil
"	22/4/17		Inspected horses 57 F Coy RE 29 under strength 2 for evacuation 17 mops. Conn Management now good the	Nil

T2134. Wt. W708-776. 500000. 4/15. Sir J. C. & S.

Army Form C. 2118.

WAR DIARY
or
INTELLIGENCE SUMMARY.

(Erase heading not required.)

ADMS. 58th Division

Instructions regarding War Diaries and Intelligence Summaries are contained in F. S. Regs., Part II. and the Staff Manual respectively. Title pages will be prepared in manuscript.

Place	Date	Hour	Summary of Events and Information	Remarks and references to Appendices
ACHIET LE GRAND	21/4/17		With DADOS interview ADOS & CAC.	
			Arranged for clothing horses on urgent needs of remainder some of Pomt from GS. Supple. Farmer is manager by Z Army. Arrangements for clothing horses & equipment to injuring of other mounted forces.	
			With DADOS investigate demands for & supply of recently received reinforcements & OR horses. The average were of horses too low. I per month. Officers say horses need finishing and induced effort of heavy work & bad weather while Batteries continuing mobility Hd.	
	22/4/17		Inspect 511 T.C. RE. After evacuation, horses in poor condition require more exercise 206 to General 47 Inch 7 horses - watery, purging & serious rangement. 2 Brigade Commanders CRA ADMS, CRE abserve the remedy of otter knowledge as with of system for remedy & horse tied back on tree of mouth. Admd where published for veto attendance on units in accordance with regd. Bryr. Group orders.	Ap.
			Inspect hors rest section regimental camp and average convection 26 horses. Horses no forms drawn inspect 509. 511 Co. NTC.	Ap.
"	23/4/17		CRA recommend improvement to detail of posting PA horses. Inspect sick animals of NRS and their attendance.	Ap.

Army Form C. 2118.

WAR DIARY
or
INTELLIGENCE SUMMARY.
(Erase heading not required.)

ANTS 58th Division

Place	Date	Hour	Summary of Events and Information	Remarks and references to Appendices
ACHIET LE GRAND	24/4/17		Visit to Mobile Sect. inspected 510 & 512 Coys A.S.C.	
			B/Y and inspected horses Transport lines 175 Inf Bgd. Animals 1/g 62nd Regt. V. Good 2/10 Good S/n some improvement. General "musing poor" 2/15 fair. Good.	S/n
	25/4/17		Inspected horses 574 & Co R.E. 2 poor remainder much improved condition. One q good 2/2 H.C. Trel Stock. Cmg q animals improved, some much improved fitting	
"			Stores from BERTRANCOURT to (for two days - 27 miles a day. Report to D.T.O. a Bde Comdr. Reported to D.T.O. a Govt. Remount Stores - Much below strength 7 horses fr Evacuation. 35 others unfit for duty. General condition good & they should not be used for heavy work or long journeys.	
"	26/4/17		Inspect the sick animals 290 Sqn. Army RFA arrange for evacuation 11 and Treatment of 12 by not half sickmen. Organize sanitary arrangements for sick animals & others not the Division. Inspect animals under treatment and advise as to Evacuation to BVSG tomorrow.	

H Turnpike Major
t SVO 27/4/17

Army Form C. 2118.

WAR DIARY
or
INTELLIGENCE SUMMARY.
(Erase heading not required.)

ADMS 58th Div.

Place	Date	Hour	Summary of Events and Information	Remarks and references to Appendices
ACHIET LE GRAND	27/4/17		Weather & roads continue good. Bring to notice of Staff Capt. 12A. that progress in erection of DS horses is not satisfactory, no hutting commenced in large lines, also not known when if ever normal line, 3/3 Battalions ten no knowledge as use of stuff suitable & when Brigade tts animals. 2/4 Battalions have not been & evacuees for 3 days — (one trunks) Submit to ADMS I Army Weekly state as follows Remaining 146 Committed 295 Total 441 Enured 136 Evacuated 58 Died 11 Destroyed 13 Remaining 281 Total 441 Strength shown 3412 mules 960 Total 3372. Organize NCOs for Brands to qualify men capable of grooming etc per obtaining and arrange for men to go from units to school of farming & tony mule up to 150). of amphous trained men. Intel return forwarded to Ensure arms, clothing, saddlery & equipment with all generals & served with him. Photograph what for organization, drums & bits taught for Trans' of sick animals not subjected	
BIRCOURT CAMP	28/4/17			
"	29/4/17		Inspect sick times—transport lines 173 Inf Regt — scale not know 173 Lord Regt. n cooperation of Stretchers	

Army Form C. 2118.

WAR DIARY
or
INTELLIGENCE SUMMARY.
(Erase heading not required.)

Instructions regarding War Diaries and Intelligence Summaries are contained in F.S. Regs, Part II. and the Staff Manual respectively. Title pages will be prepared in manuscript.

Place	Date	Hour	Summary of Events and Information	Remarks and references to Appendices
ACHIET le GRAND	30/4/17		Horse 261 7/3 Lond Regt destroyed for Chronic glanders. Transport sprayed & Capt? mineral and inserted with special wash treatment. Gallery Car of Brigade completed during respective or emergency care. Sanitary measures completed for affected unit. Isolation in hand for Brigade to preclude recognition of any case. No initiation and measures adopted to prevent spreading of disease by contact & or not change of bivouac or other gear. DDVS visited encamped or A.V.Hd. on formation of next Corps Anti Myrolistin from all Divisions in the Corps ADVS were instructed that school 58 Educa & arrangy to had to supply (i.e. next Formation ACorp. 2 men (with training as Check).	
Biehucourt Camp	1/5/17		ADVS Corps postulated for isolation of any animal having completed symptoms of glanders and measures to prevent spread of disease. Monitoring care & making sin Inspect out animals. Transport lines 175 Inf Bng. Recommend more training and more serious men + pack & draught work and one boy to walk. Pry Transport full furnace	
"	2/5/17		Inspect out animals. Transport lines 174 Inf (Regt Group. Animals all improvement on 2/6 7/3 Lond Regt. Recommendations cancelled & those 175 Brigade	
"	3/5/17		Inspect Sick remounts moving to Divarm at AVELUY enroute for Central supervision of two apparently healthy but slightly other horses going to DAC	

Army Form C. 2118.

WAR DIARY
or
INTELLIGENCE SUMMARY.
(Erase heading not required.)

Instructions regarding War Diaries and Intelligence Summaries are contained in F. S. Regs., Part II. and the Staff Manual respectively. Title pages will be prepared in manuscript.

Place	Date	Hour	Summary of Events and Information	Remarks and references to Appendices
ACHIET L. GRAND (BIHUCOURT CAMP)	2/5/17		Inspect horse 3½ and 2/2 H.C. Jambulances considerable improvement	
	3/5/17		DVS and TDVS inspected Horses 5/my 5/th G. FLD. Amb. Considerable & most approved. Matters took up all time in the Common brought service from England to complete and reported without question so adequacy reasoning - DDV. Inspect horses in Aug Co (much improved) and horses in common in hand by Sec Letter to D.H.D. forwarded by too as circular to HQ of formation - That D more surveys, work having the brought so pack animals is required to meet demands for M future work of Standard. If work were to established to knew beyond which demand must not be made; one is urgent I am willing operations where T.Os. and other officers in charge of horses must carry out orders with report security that report the work is overrun.	½
"	4/5/17		Weekly State submitted to DDVS. I army as follows: Remaining 218 Admitted 116 Total 334 Jaured 86 Transfered 50 Died 4 Destroyed 8 Remaining 186 Total 334 Strength Horses 26627 Mules 915 Total 3542 Visit Wagon Lines R.A.	½
"	5/5/17		Inspect bottom watering ception R.A. Lines BEHAGNIES, ERVILLERS, E.P.H.VILLERS. Read.	½

WAR DIARY or INTELLIGENCE SUMMARY

Army Form C. 2118.

Place	Date	Hour	Summary of Events and Information	Remarks and references to Appendices
BIHUCOURT CAMP	5/5/17		Investigate routine of horse management R.A. Brigade Lines morning & evening. Animals appear to be getting both grooming & rug off.	
ACHIET LE GRAND	6/5/17		No exercise was looking to water and management problem or grazing while driven horses are exchanging hay – Stationary A.M.D. ADMS & C.R.A. on discovery organisation to improve arrangement for horse above – and report that progress in condition of animals is most satisfactory. Establishment not yet reached by 5 horses transferred to R.A. (when states)	JFG JFG
"	7/5/17		At MAILLY MAILLET inspect horse – under D.A.A. & Q.M.G. and D.D.V.S. & imporved. At ACHEUX inspected transport 2/3 H.C. Field Ambulance. Animals much improved by rest & reorganisation & more exercise & training now required the hospital lines considerable work (after excellent brothers over 30/4/17) have been muddy – abilities depot & big number of sick animals in 510 B.V.S.H whose position is unsatisfactory. Point out it not wanting arrangement an unsatisfactory arrangement	JFG
"	8/5/17		require better exercise & grooming – Employ system inadequate stay & early improved H.Q. with Officer in charge Battery wagon lines 291 Bty R.F.A. Urge the necessity of more exercise & training for horses, better organisation of routine, walking fodder & many horses stand wanting back & shoulder skins health, inadequate opportunity	
"	9/5/17			

WAR DIARY or INTELLIGENCE SUMMARY

Army Form C. 2118.

ADVS 58(?) Div[?]

Place	Date	Hour	Summary of Events and Information	Remarks and references to Appendices
BIHUCOURT CAMP	9/5/17		of good grazing now available. Grooming requires further organization reduced horses. stable hours should be increased whilst horses shown lighter work and more care taken of animals with skin cold suffering from dermatitis due to exposure in first bad weather	H.G.
ACHIET LE GRAND	10/5/17		With officer of Battery hospital here 340 Bty RFA is about suspect sick animals under treatment at host they destine [?] considerable improvement in work of the unit	J.W.
"	11/5/17		For evacuation of our 20 patient. Work by plate submitted to 300 V Army as follows Remaining 184 Admitted 9, total 253 Cured 52 Destroyed 16 Died 10 Destroyed 8 missing 6 Remaining 169 total 25. strength horses 2618 mules 906 total 3524. Submit to CPA. 1 rt 341 Bde (?) 13/Lthrys horses better harnessed, grooming + [?] 10 regiment amongst RA horses	J.W.A.
"	12/5/17		Re army mules, mule they best and order mastication of men not typhoid terms	H.G.
"	13/5/17		Inspect 85 remounts arriving for the Division at BAPAUME	H.G.
"	14/5/17		At FAVREUIL inspect animals 510 Co ASC much improved. animals still require more work. army shooting reserve in rear of the line of completed range concealed	H.G.

WAR DIARY or INTELLIGENCE SUMMARY

Army Form C. 2118.

Place	Date	Hour	Summary of Events and Information	Remarks and references to Appendices
ACHIET-L-GRAND Bihucourt Camp	14/5/17		Inspect 512 Co ASC much improved - inoculat[ion] 2 horses / debility / good / postal break- ammunition attd report more services	
			50B FC RE at work SAPIGNIES 2 cases hands [hospital] with sprained & wounded remained improving, one nothing only horses on duty storm	
"	15/5/17		Attend L. HQrs for Confce Cmdg arrangements for days time to concentrate, watering & horses from village ponds to forbidden, men with empty repaired BIHUCOURT, organizn of watering compound ACHIET L GRAND work improvement, all times water troughs should be emptied & cleaned nightly, burn kitchen rubbish on open compound, sanitation, latrines & harnessing horses two then when opened in much building throughout village	
			Organizing the distribution of anti gas respirators to troops in Division as follows 1st Battery 60 SMC section 70 DAC Balr 50 Bny HQ (2f) & 1cSm Co 37. 3 Co ASC 16.	/h.
"	16/5/17		Inspect early morning watering RA & SAC. Inspect arrival 175 Dy Bny Group. Considerable improvement - 3" Hod Regt. Inspect host btty DAC Some times under treatment not making apparent progress.	/h,
"	17/5/17		arrange for evacuation of ones others to to post on special natures organise rechednulation of route duties of Dream during evening term of shower & hot dry feel	/h

WAR DIARY or INTELLIGENCE SUMMARY

Army Form C. 2118.
A.D.V.S. 58th Div.

Place	Date	Hour	Summary of Events and Information	Remarks and references to Appendices
ACHIET LE GRAND	18/5/17		Capt. Scott Bowden A.V.C. to command Mob. Vet. Sect. during 10 days absence Capt. Richmond M.C.	
Bihucourt Camp			In reply to E. Army - submit that R.A. horses requiring exit. troop & grooping, for 2 to 3 hrs between watering, & the pri horse for other work possible without causing loss of horses. General orders for reduction should be dependent not only on grass available but location of camps - that concentration of horses, work & hours, and time is not available at any one particular...	
			Weekly stat. forwarded to DDVS I Army as follows. Remounting 18g Admitted 93. Total 262. Issued 103. Evacuated 19. Died 6 destroyed & Remaining 130. Total 262. Strength horses 2582 mules 942 Total 3504 Casualties 4pc	
			Percentage of wastage informed joint Sheets – 9/1, 2/7, 1.8/, 1/7, .83/7	
	19/5/17		Inspect horses 290 Bay RFA with Remount Officer I Corps T/02210 Sergt P.H.IL.IPS A.V.C. unmounted out. 291 Bay RFA not bad condy. Bony & notes the improvement required in	
			carts harness, anxiety over no means of horses knees enlarged – informed that time not employed & indifferent opportunity taken of good grazing available – suggest daily return to be rendered approved for "morning break".	
	20/5/17		Submit to DMP. CRA change of routine & improvement required in horses 290 Bay RFA	
			Recommend to DHQ. Artillery unit to concentrate to Harm grazing fresh oxygen Brigades (Wagon lines) etc.	

WAR DIARY / INTELLIGENCE SUMMARY

Army Form C. 2118.

ADJT. S/Lt Brown

Place	Date	Hour	Summary of Events and Information	Remarks and references to Appendices
Achiet le Grand Bihucourt Camp	20/5/17		We moved for this reason. In reply to II Army letter asking why number of sick/debility/exhaustion cases so high as compared with cog. ANZAC CORPS:- (1) All divisions II Corps very high as apparently the condition of two corps not comparable. (2) 80%. of cases S.E. Divs. from R.A. have just arrived in deplorable state, without essential Egypt. medical equipment arrived in deplorable condition. — a condition of 17th Div. (3) Running turnover output from tropical zones of Divisions especially in transfer to II Army when it was notified to 15th D. 15 Divs III Army. There would be huge wastage from a condition of animals.	21/4/17
	21/5/17		Inspect animals 57 NFA. No 2 section very good. No 3 sect. much improved, no good. No 1 Sect. generally good — more shoe covers required by animals in 3 sect. remember next... strokes for improvement of ration. Arrangts for evacuation to cases from most LF Stat. to BASE. Capt A. Reid ARC to 291 Brig. RA invalided out. His duties arranged for	Itc.
	22/5/17		Inspect 158 remount cavalry for Division at BAPAUME	Itc.
	23/5/17		Visit horse lines and inspect sick animals 503 TC RE & 175 Siege Bty Group	Itc.

WAR DIARY or INTELLIGENCE SUMMARY

Army Form C. 2118.

ADMS 58th Division

Place	Date	Hour	Summary of Events and Information	Remarks and references to Appendices
ACHIET LE GRAND Bihucourt Camp	23/5/17		Inspect horses 504 & 511 Field Cos R.E. Former shew little change, latter somewhat improved. Arrang for 3 to go to next Tech- Adv. Tr. h......on for evacuation. Inspect wounds 2/1 H.C. Field Ambulance. 511 C.R.F.C. considerably improved. Attend instruction on orders for reporting for horses by Maj. Gen. Green to N.C.Os (and available officers) from all units both Transport and available officers) and walked through. Completed to 73rd Lond. Regt. on cooperation of Divls from occurrence of Clinical Jaundice- Copy of all served to SASOs and above Brigade. Had notice time on visit may be relied.	Ap.
"	24/5/17		Inspect remounts—29.03.17— and work. Regiment line given of that Brigade regarding duty return of horses to improve their service. Morning in Marshall's for forging (Capt R.W. GLAISTER M.C. admitted with 9/3 H.C. Field Ambulance (osteomyelitis scrofuleux F.C.C.S.) re-arrange with Doctor. Capt TAYLOR Att. 70/R.A. vice SCOTT BOWDEN in charge of tuck room and commanding Mot. Kit Sec. Forward man work by A.D.V.S. Inspect sick animals. M. Hughes arranges for .... of h. Inspect horses 509 Co. A.T.C. considerably improved — to except for duty. Men & Lubricants to desinfectin must be obtained as soon as more too painful in open. So Finished in open.	Ap.

WAR DIARY or INTELLIGENCE SUMMARY.

Army Form C. 2118.

Place	Date	Hour	Summary of Events and Information	Remarks and references to Appendices
AOH.ET.L.6 GARD Belmont Camp	25/5/17		Weekly state of sick animals submitted to DDVS. L Army as follows. Remaining 130. Admitted 107. Total 237. Cured 63. Transferred 36. Died 2. Destroyed 9. (Casualties) (remains) Remaining 104. Incoming 3. Total 237. own strength. Strength Horses 2475 mules 1016. Total 3491 own. Inspected horses 73 7 Ank. much improved. Have kept horse working in ambulance 7/5 7 Ank. relieved no work at B & A A 4 M I E S. Reported by telegram DVS we have evacuated by W.V.S. train 24/5/17 proved at BASE VOY. hospital to be glandered. Investigate animals tracing and against recurring [illegible]. Animal proved 5th on strength W.V. STC (3rd station) for no they. when [illegible] to held H.Q. Vet 18/5/17. Only in current monthly not lot dest. entered at rear. Submit by telephone rates. SAPS L Army Phones to deal with this infection of Glanders —	2/6
"	26/5/17		(1) STC to have no restrictions as normal animals regularly exhibited for period in their lives (2) All possible contacts ie in lot dest. to be segregated for 21 days as of past have one of clinical glanders at time of evacuation. Notify W. 7 BASE VET. H. of animal evacuated 24/5/17 own specials in contact for [illegible] dup with Case above which be honoured. To plan in contact sent to Army C.out. Stare with [illegible] have applied of which to see full details.	2/6

WAR DIARY or INTELLIGENCE SUMMARY

Army Form C. 2118.

ADVS 58th Division

Instructions regarding War Diaries and Intelligence Summaries are contained in F.S. Regs., Part II. and the Staff Manual respectively. Title pages will be prepared in manuscript.

(Erase heading not required.)

Place	Date	Hour	Summary of Events and Information	Remarks and references to Appendices
ACHIET LE GRAND Billets and Camps	26/5/17		Visit surgeon lines 291 Bty RFA. horse adjudant & wagon line greens improve in all the vicinity & all horses being properly harnessed & trimmed for work by privates building, the grooming although improved is indifferent, animals with dirty skins must be sweated. There is some improvement in orgying stun of horse rations & vould use better H.R. Visit sick animals BSMP Div Sgn Co + 313 FC Fort (immediate) + horses & Fort stripped at Puirits yesterday) 148 M Gun Co + 175 Div Emp Group. Weather throughout the period generally good — and grooming pairs been provided. Excellent grooming for prev 3 weeks, morale good.	JR.

J.H. Crawfield
Major,
A.D.V.S.
58th (LONDON) DIVISION.

Confidential

[Stamp: 58th (LONDON) DIVISION — Date 1/8/17 — (VETERINARY)]

H.Q.
  58th Division

Herewith please find War DIARY
  I ADVS. 58th Divn.
  II OC 2/1 London Mob Vety Sect.

for period 27/5/17 – 31/5/17 to complete
past months in accordance with
instructions.

H Crawford, Major,
A.D.V.S.
58th (LONDON) DIVISION.

ADHQ.
2·6·17

Army Form C. 2118.
40.

WAR DIARY
or
INTELLIGENCE SUMMARY.
(Erase heading not required.)

A.D.S. 58th Division

Place	Date	Hour	Summary of Events and Information	Remarks and references to Appendices
ACHIET LE GRAND Advanced Camp	27/5/17		Inspect arrivals 2/1 J.K. Field. Condition good - arrange for evacuation & charge.	HH
	28/5/17		Arrange cook mews in foretold M.V. Sect. Inspect cook views stabled at B/140 Coop RE. organize sanitation measures for M.V.Sect. — and for each Inf Bdy JHG. whose harries have occupied inspected stable. Inspected arrivals & contacts wounded & BAH. Sick admitted. Closed. Visit sick animals 175 Inf Bdy. - (Sure sick on mule frost: central rattles from gun shot wound.) 174 Inf Bdy. Inspect horses JHO 173 . 174 Inf Bdy. Report B.H.P. with Frenchs. R.A. area not of repair. repair & supply replaced urgently. Visit sick 512 C.A.S.C. - arrange for evacuation & supply obtain cross A.S.91 R.F.A. 1 Inf Sect. S.A.C	HH
"	29.5.17		A.M.S. open moves to M.D.S. Capt RICHMOND M.C. posted to S.9. Barry RFA (on return from leave) Capt SCOTT. BOWDEN A.V.C in command of "A" And M.D.S. M.S.Y. Sect. Inspect Remounts arrived by train BAPAUME. Visit sick animals 510. 512 CAASC	HH
MORY.	30.5.17		Inspect Re Remount arriving by train BAPAUME. Inspect arrivals 175 Inf Bdy. Divnl Sig Co - groomy & construct of batter indifferent in charge of system recommended. A209 took on cuts - grooming excellent. A 291	HH
"	31.5.17		Inspect horses 290 . 291. Bmp. RFA. report BSMD battn. much improved B 291. much more efficient after improved command	HH

Army Form C. 2118.

WAR DIARY
or
INTELLIGENCE SUMMARY. A.V.I. 58th Divn

(Erase heading not required.)

Place	Date	Hour	Summary of Events and Information	Remarks and references to Appendices
MORY	31/8/17		Report to DHQ re horses 2 g.o. Bay RFA. B Battery improved under new routine. D Battery much improved. C Battery in contact now & all other units in Division show an improvement in stabling - horses on B Battery still too dirty & horses unfit for duty. Arrange for inoculation 11 horses from in V.P. Sect. after general inspection	
			Moss 2/9/17	

K Crawfield Major
AVS 58th Divn

Army Form C. 2118.

WAR DIARY
or
INTELLIGENCE SUMMARY.
(Erase heading not required.)

ADMS 58th Div.

Place	Date	Hour	Summary of Events and Information	Remarks and references to Appendices
MORY.	1.6.17.		Submit a proposal which is approved by ADMS II Corps that larger units RA drawn to supplies with Potalkin utensils & portable cooking of Leari kids. new of high value — links in the field unable to market canteen. Recommend to DDMS that as many L.D. troops for RA arriving from Remounts as possible, come to would to Potalkins to prevent formal opening of Triangle in DAH of front horse troops DAC also take all trouble. It would give Batty: Commanders some avocados from their troops might be saved for broken horses expelled by VRA in lines - Batty horses are not accustomed to mule.	
"	"		Weekly state submitted — DDMS III Army sent to follow. — Remaining 104 Admitted 152. To Col 306. To work 64. Transferred to sick & Discharged 2 Coming 124 In total 306. Strength Horses 2705 mules 1127. To Col 3632. Sickbirdstay '627.	4/z
MORY.	2/6/17. 3.6.17.		Inspected remounts arriving by train from BAPAUME. Investigate death of mule suspected of contagious ophtha and several milder cases of that type. DAC inspecting all suspects of the nature (no 3) & removal of the same batch. Find no signs of specific disease.	10/z 11/z
"	4/6/17.		Emerald on suspected mange cow from width of 1/1st HCFA. 3/11 cattle &c. Sanitary measures to unit concerned.	12/z

Army Form C. 2118.

(43)

A.D.V.S. 58th Div.

WAR DIARY
or
INTELLIGENCE SUMMARY.
(Erase heading not required.)

Instructions regarding War Diaries and Intelligence Summaries are contained in F.S. Regs., Part II. and the Staff Manual respectively. Title pages will be prepared in manuscript.

Place	Date	Hour	Summary of Events and Information	Remarks and references to Appendices
MORY	5/6/17		Report to D.H.Q. transferring of watering arrangements for RA horses over 3 troughs ERNVILLERS - BEHAGNIES Rd worn out. Visit ADSs 174 Div .112 had Kit feet - a probable interchange of level work & areas. Inspect 2/1 F.C. Ambulance. Arranging with site for next HQ Stat. which lies nearly too crippled to shell fire.	
	6/6/17	Visit sick animals 174th Bgde Horses of 290 BrigRCA. Horses B 291 appear to be getting fast reduce to sane cases - other battries 291 horses doing well. Inspect animals ho! Sect DAC. which are improved by transfer to & from work & Batteries also by little work in reserve. Services & recharge still capable of improvement. CAPT M.REID1 AVC. evacuated to BASE, has temporary sickness P.V.O. now designated MALARIA. Inspect march D.H.Q.	17Ah. 17Ah. 17Ah.
	8/6/17	Submit weekly stat. to DDVS III Army Smith as follows. Remaining 121 admitted 112 Total 233 Cured 92 Evacuated 34 Died 5 Destroyed 3 Remaining 119. Total 242 = 2. Strength Horses 2822 mules 1148 Total 3970. Evacuated mule, 757.	
	9.6.17	Visit units 173 Bgde Group - and 17 Div Brigade	17Ah.
	10.6.17	Inspect sick animals 174 Bty Pony. SAA.D. and 2/2 J.C. Fand 7/3/F.C. Ambulance.	17Ah.

T2134. Wt. W708—776. 500000. 4/15. Sir J. C. & S.

WAR DIARY
or
INTELLIGENCE SUMMARY.
(Erase heading not required.)

Army Form C. 2118.

A.T.V.S 58th Division

(44)

Place	Date	Hour	Summary of Events and Information	Remarks and references to Appendices
MORY	11/6/17		Inspect horses for evacuation from Mottershead	/tk
"	12/6/17		Inspect horses + sick 291 Bony R.F.A. Sick animals has lost stuff	/tk
			126 Remount arrives at BAPAUME condition good - all apparently healthy	
"	13.6.17		Inspect horses 510 - 511 512 ASC Cos: Those of the latter much improved	/tk
"	14.6.17		—	/tk
"	15.6.17		Call on Col. PARLIN K5VS. III Army at ALBERT for instruction under new army.	/tk
			Weekly Stats submitted to DDVS. III Army on gitters - Remaining 119 admitted by Army	
"	16/6		Total 206 August 72 Transferred 33 Died nil Destroyed 2 Missing nil Total 1139	
			Total 206 Strength horses 2957 mules 1144. Total 4101.	
"	16.6.17		Inspect horses 290 Bony R.F.A. from improvement B.C Battn	/tk
"	17.6.17		Visit Capt. GLAISTER ATV into at S.G.S. COLINCAMPS. find here evacuated 1/3980	/tk
			Report to DDVS for him to be replaced - Inspect sick 174 Bony	
			Dummy for evacuation of unfit - have mostly mange.	
"	18.6.17		Heavy thunderstorms - rain - Horses have very miserable but much not affected	/tk
"	19.6.17		Inspect transport horses, Annex 173 Bry Br, 51 Hund Regt Survey + good	/tk
"	20.6.17		2/10 21/12 R Regt 2/9 topo3 B1 good 2/9 Regiment horses seem less. Showing hay fed 1/2 lbs 13mo 175 7M B	
				/tk

WAR DIARY
or
INTELLIGENCE SUMMARY.

ADYS. 58th Div.

Army Form C. 2118.

Place	Date	Hour	Summary of Events and Information	Remarks and references to Appendices
MORY.	21/6/19		Inspected sick arrival at not by Stat for evacuation, not bad. No/sick. BMC and sick horses S.P Army Troops	1A
"	22/6/19		Weekly State submitted to ADMS. III Army as follows. Remaining 109. Admitted 96. Total 205. Cured 6. Invalided 23. Died 1. Discharged 1. Remaining 2. Remaining 119. Total 209. Strength 2439. India 1143. Total 4065. Percentage of invaliding weekly through ill health 58th Division .6%, 75-7. 41). 39%. Interior of S.T.H.s and work, that after horses have been approximately independent during the trains which undergoing odd checks & covers, and take arrivals disposed for protection from enemy, in moves to trick more yards & trucks & should be stimulated by great change in trying out I have know & appearance of animals.	1A
"	23.6.19		Admen received for me to proceed to 8 D.V.S. an ADSVS accompanying them	
"	24.6.19		ISHQ moves to COURCELLES	
COURCELLES	25.6.19.		Stand over duties of DADVS 58th Divs to Capt. SCOTT ROBDEN.	J.H.

H. Crompton Maj. MC.
ADVS 58th Div.

WAR DIARY
or
INTELLIGENCE SUMMARY.
(Erase heading not required.)

D.A.D.V.S
58th Div.

Army Form C. 2118.

(46)

Place	Date	Hour	Summary of Events and Information	Remarks and references to Appendices
COURCELLES	25.6.17		Major H. GREENFIELD A.V.C. left 6.30 to 3rd Division. Assumed duties as D.A.D.V.S. on appointment. Capt. M.O. GWYNN A.V.C. (S.R.) reported for duty & posted as V.O. 1/2 Div Train attached to B.11 Coy A.S.C. A.D.V.S Corps & D.H.Q. notified. Evacuated sick animals at M.V.S. for Pneumonia.	J.V.B
"	26.6.17		Superintended entraining of 27 sick animals from M.V.S. at ACHIET LE GRAND Station. Mule died over Spiers field Vety Hosp. to Capt. GWYNN.	S.V.B
"	27.6.17		Met Capts. GWYNN & TAYLOR J2. to arrange the works. Application received for release of Sergt. ATTENBORO' H.R.C. attached to 173 Inf. Bde for farm work at home. Application forwd. R.H.Q. Visited D.C. of 1/12.13th Hus. reference evacuation of his Charger. Pending arrival of 2 more Officers am continuing test on M.V.S. Visited O.C. 58. D.A.C. to enquire of Horses suddenly from Buttmanshill Vety. Christophers left by Capt. R. GLAISTER A.V.C are still in possession found all in order.	S.C.h.
"	28.6.17		Received letter from A.D.V.S. I Corps. with instructions to infect A/291 R.F.A. & 2/9 London Regt. with regard to recent mange outbreak, probably this Infected A/291 R.F.A. found all ranks of mange Supplies, have come from Right Section had 4 their sufficient cases isolated & gave all necessary directions as to precautions to taking isolation of Battery	S.V.B

WAR DIARY
or
INTELLIGENCE SUMMARY.

Army Form C. 2118.

D.A.D.V.S
58" Div

(7)

Place	Date	Hour	Summary of Events and Information	Remarks and references to Appendices
COURCELLES	28.6.17		Cont². Visited watering Sect. Selected sick animals for evacuation. Paid the men.	eff.
"	29.6.17		Inspected 2/9 London Regt. & 2/2 M.C. Field Amb. In former unit found the case of mange had been a stray animal which was sent into M.V.S., & re-examined. I could not observe any trace of mange in the unit. Forwarded report to D.D.V.S. F Corps upon the result of my inspection of 2/9 L.R.F.A. & 2/9 London Regt. Epizootic Lymphangitis continuing evacuation M/H Sick animals from M.V.S at ACHIET LE GRAND Station. Weekly conference of V.O.s present Capts RICHMOND, TAYLOR & GWYNN. Weekly state submitted to D.D.V.S III Army & A.D.V.S Corps as follows. Remaining 119. Admitted 102. Total 221. Cured 71. Transferred & Base Hospital 33. Died 2. Destroyed 4. Remaining 111. Total 221. Strength Horses 2939 Mules 1135. Total 4074. % Mess Loss for Div.¹ 0.68%. Inspected 291 Brigade R.F.A. Routine duties at office, M.V.S.	eff. SW3 SW3
"	30.6.17			

W.H. Burwell Sir
Capt - Div
D.A.D.V.S
58 Div

Army Form C. 2118.

D.A.D.V.S.
58th Div.

WAR DIARY
or
INTELLIGENCE SUMMARY
(Erase heading not required.)

Instructions regarding War Diaries and Intelligence Summaries are contained in F.S. Regs., Part II. and the Staff Manual respectively. Title pages will be prepared in manuscript.

Place	Date	Hour	Summary of Events and Information	Remarks and references to Appendices
COURCELLES	1/7/17		Rebooked A.D.V.S. V Corps. Accompanied him on inspection of A Batty. 291 Bgde. R.F.A. 7 animals sutlicast. 6 animals evacuated as suspected. Sergt. P.C. ATTENBOROUGH A.V.C attached 173 Inf. Bgde. granted 1 month special leave to work on land at home, Attached W.O. /c Base Records for temporary replacement.	L/3
"	2/7/17		Inspected 174 Inf. Bgde. Div.mm.P. D.H.Q. 509 Coy A.S.C. 9 animals for evacuation at M.V.S	L/3
"	3/7/17		Superintended evacuation of sick animals from M.V.S. at ACHIET LES GRAND Station. Inspected 290 & 291 Bgdes R.F.A. Visited new area, found many thin animals. Capt. T.B. TAYLOR A.V.C reported for duty & Field V.A.G. Arranged move of M.V.S. to new area to take over from 42nd Div M.V.S. at ROCQUIGNY on 9.7.17.	L/3
"	4/7/17		Notified A.D.V.S. V Corps movement of Div. artillery & D.A.C. to new areas. Capt./S. RICHMOND, TAYLOR,T.B. & TAYLOR,J.L. A.V.C. accompanying these units.	L/3
"	5/7/17		Visited 42nd Div. H.Q. at YERES. 4.M.V.S. site at ROCQUIGNY very extreme, uneven ground, not good. Lot close to motor troughs, & dust bad. Arranged tall over tentage.	L/3
"	6/7/17		Inspected sick animals for evacuation at M.V.S Superintended evacuation of sick animals at ACHIET. LES GRAND. M/Tyred A.D.V.S V Corps of Div. move from area.	L/3
"	7/7/17		Inspected Div Sig. Coy. D.H.Q., R.E.H.Q., 2/2 H.C.F.A. Arranged details of M.V.S. move.	L/3

WAR DIARY or INTELLIGENCE SUMMARY

Army Form C. 2118.

DAP VS
D. DW
58

Place	Date	Hour	Summary of Events and Information	Remarks and references to Appendices
COURCELLES	2.7.17		Cavl: Weekly returns forwarded in duplicate to 32 & III Army troops F.A.D.V.S. & Q.M.G. Showing Remaining 110, admitted 90, T/Md 190, Cured 65, Transferred Sick 26, Died nil, Destroyed nil, missing nil, Remaining 99. T/Md 190. Strength Horses 2537, Mules 1187. T/Md 4024. Wastage 0.84%.	LApp
"	8.7.17		Forage return received 15th ratios 9-2lbs Hay per horse. Capt. C.H. SHEATHER R.C. reported for duty on appointment as O.C. 15" Div. M.V.S. Same handed over to him. F Corps received by VI Corps. Substituted for DVS VI Corps. Accompanied him on inspection of MVS. Mobile Div. S.C.O. on unofficiency of Bream.	LApp
YPRES	9.7.17		Div.H.Q. moved from COURCELLES. M.V.S. moved from BIHUCOURT to ROCQUIGNY. Inspected Camp. Found all left clean & tidy.	SApp
"	10.7.17		Inspected M.V.S. rearranged camp arrangements, gave orders for permanent horse standings to be made, followed administration of 42nd Div. Artillery 2 DAC (210 & 211 Bydes R.F.A.)	LApp
"	11.7.17		Inspected Div. Artillery animals generally in poor condition reported accordingly to A.Q. called for full ration forage for them.	LApp, SApp
"	12.7.17		Inspected A.S.C. Companies, 2/1 & 2/3 H.C.T.D.	SApp
"	13.7.17		Conference A.D.Os present Capts. RICHMOND, TAYLOR, EVANS, TAYLOR.T.E, SHEATHER, LORD.H.H. V.Os 210 Byde R.F.A. and AUXTON 10/c 211 Byde R.F.A. Weekly returns in triplicate forwarded	LApp

Army Form C. 2118.

WAR DIARY
or
INTELLIGENCE SUMMARY.
(Erase heading not required.)

D.A.D.V.S.
S.S D.W
50

Place	Date	Hour	Summary of Events and Information	Remarks and references to Appendices
YPRES.	13.7.17	Cont'd	to A.D.V.S. IV Corps showing Remaining 99. Admitted 82. Well 181. Cured 47. Transferred S/K 23. Died nil, Destroyed 5. Remaining 107. Total 181. Mousing 8. Strength Horses 2967, Mules 1256/Mules 4123. Wastage 0.67%.	49/3
"	14.7.17		Attended conference of D.D.V.S. at office of A.D.V.S IV Corps, GREVILLERS. Submitted cases for evacuation at M.V.S. Still forage ration granted to Artillery Horses IV Corps 12.5/10. R.	48/3
"	15.7.17		Capt. H.H. LORD, A.V. VC/c 210 Bde R.F.A. left for "Orlings Leave to England, duties taken over by Capt. QUILTON. Inspected 290, 291 Bde R.F.A. Transferred 42 animals debilitated horses for evacuation.	49/3
"	16.7.17		Inspected 2/3 H.F.A. 507, 511 & 512 Coys A.S.C. Submitted animals for evacuation at M.V.S. Inspection of M.V.S. by The Div Commander Major Genl A.D. FANSHAWE. C.B. who expressed satisfaction with the Camp & condition of The Section Horses. Also scrutinised the evacuation of the debilitated aged animals 42 in number from the Div Artillery.	51/3
"	17.7.17		Inspected N° 2 Sect 42nd D.A.C discovered 3 positive & 3 suspected cases of mange, Malsanne Sent to M.V.S. Inspected 211 Bde R.F.A. found 16 cases of suspected mange. A.D.V.S IV Corps notified by letter P.1.Ale/Mange, also C.R.A. 42nd Div. Arranged inspection by A.D.V.S IV Corps of 211 Bde R.F.A. for 11 a.m. 18.7.17.	52/3
"	18.7.17		Accompanied A.D.V.S IV C/s/c in inspection of 211 Bde R.F.A. 20 suspect mange cases evacuated to M.V.S	52/3

WAR DIARY or INTELLIGENCE SUMMARY

Army Form C. 2118.

DADVS
56 2/

Place	Date	Hour	Summary of Events and Information	Remarks and references to Appendices
YPRES	18.7.17	Cont'd	W/A/Serjt. HAYES. J. A.V.C. arrived from No. 23 Vet. Hospital for temporary duty with 173 Inf/y Bgde vice Serjt. ATTENBOROUGH	228
"	19.7.17		Visited 290 & 291 Bdes R.F.A. Inspected 33 Remounts on arrival at PERONNE from DIEPPE. 2 Suspect Mange very itchy lesions in Skin, one 18 years old, 2 very poor in condition & one bad Catarrh. Serjt. COTTAM. 3E/863 reported sick for duty & completed establishment	293
"	20.7.17		Conference D.D.O's present. Capts. RICHMOND, GLYNN, TAYLOR, TAYLOR J.C. & BULTON. Inspected 2/10 Lond Regt H.D. horses very poor. Inspected cases for evacuation at HQrs Nearby. Returns to A.D.V.S. IV Corps. Showing Remaining 107. Admitted 136 Total 243. Evac'd 65. Transferred Sick 77. Died 2. Destroyed 2. Remaining 97 Total 243. Strength – Horses 2544 Mules 1227 Total 4083. Wastage 1.9 %.	294
"	21.7.17		Attended Conference of DDVS at Office of ADVS IV Corps ETRICOURT. Inspected remounts at 290 & 291 Bgde. Inspected iron Sectn DAC	295
"	22.7.17		Inspected R&HQ. R.E 4th M.G.C., 214 M.G.Coy, 2/10 Lond Regt. No. 2 Sect. DAC, 2/6 Lond Regt.	298
"	23.7.17		Accompanied ADVS. IV Corps in inspection of 290 & 291 Bgde R.F.A. Inspected 2/5 M.F.A. G-cases for evacuation & M.I. 5	228
"	24.7.17		Accompanied A.D.V.S. IV Corps on inspection of 175 Inf/y Bgde. 503 Coy R.E. 175 T.M. Batt'y, 2/6 Lond Regt. 214 M.G. Coy. Inspected Div Sig Coy.	228

Army Form C. 2118.

52/

WAR DIARY
or
INTELLIGENCE SUMMARY.
(Erase heading not required.)

DADVS 58th Divn

Place	Date	Hour	Summary of Events and Information	Remarks and references to Appendices
YPRES.	24.7.17	Cont.	Pte SARBEANT A.V.C. SE 9388 reported for duty with M.V.S. Vice 4/2/Corp. HAYLLAR who was admitted to Hospital in England while on Special Leave.	SOS
"	25.7.17		Inspected 290 Bde R.F.A. + 73rd Inf. Bde.	SOS
"	27.7.17		Conference of M.O's. Present:- Capts. RICHMOND, TAYLOR. I.G., GLYNN, TAYLOR. J.L., SHEATHER, & AULTON. Capt. A.H.LORD A.V.C. 210 Bde. R.F.A. reported after 10 days leave in England. A.V.S. IV Corps notified. Capt. A.H.LORD A.V.C. V.O. to be notified. Weekly returns in triplicate forwarded to ADVS. IV Corps showing:- Remaining 97 admitted 68. Total 165. Cured 85. Transferred Sick 7. Died nil. Destroyed nil. Remaining 73. Total 165. Missing nil. Strength:- Horses 2881. Mules 1242. Total 4123. Mustaps 0.1670.	SOS SOS
"	28.7.17		Attended Conference of DADVS at office of ADVS IV Corps ETRICOURT. Visited 58th DAC. Pte BRISTON clerk to DADVS departs on 10 days Special Leave to England.	SOS SOS
"	30.7.17		Visit to M.V.S. stranded cases visit No 2 Sect. 42nd DAC. Notified all V.O's to exercise all precautions to avoid occupying Standings, Stables + lines in new areas where mange has existed.	SOS SOS
"	31.7.17		D.H.Q moves to new area at FOSSEUX.	

J.W.M. Rowden
Major
DADVS
58th London Divn

31.7.17

Army Form C. 2118.

WAR DIARY or INTELLIGENCE SUMMARY.

D.A.D.V.S. 58th (London) Div

(Erase heading not required.)

Place	Date	Hour	Summary of Events and Information	Remarks and references to Appendices
FOSSEUX	1/8/17		Divisn. less artillery units in fact. Artillery remaining in YPRES area attached to 9" Divn. Notified A.D.V.S. XVII Corps of arrival in XVII Corps area. Arrange accommodation in FOSSEUX for M.V.S. Visit inspect. 41. H.C. + A. H.Q. + G. 510 Coy A.S.C.	SBB
"	2/8/17		M.V.S. arrive by road, having stayed the night at ABLAINZEVELLE & occupy new quarters at FOSSEUX. Notify A.D.V.S. XVII Corps of arrival. Direction Visit & inspect D.H.Q. Divn Sig Coy. 503, 504 + 571 Field Coys R.E. & M.M.R.	SBB
"	3.8.17		Weekly conference of V.O.'s present Capts SHEATHER & GLYNN. Weekly returns forwarded to A.D.V.S. XVII Corps Showing. Last Return 78 Admitted 17. Total 92 Cured 62. Transferred Sick 6 Died 1. Destroyed nil. Remaining 23. Total 92 Strength of horses 1278 Mules 479 Total 1757.	SBB
"	4.8.17		Visit & inspect 174 Infantry Bgde BERNEVILLE. Suspect mange case discovered in 2/6 Battn. Sent to m.v.s. for observation. 512 Coy A.S.C. Attend weekly conference at Office of A.D.V.S. XVII Corps ETRUN.	SBB
"	6.8.17		SE/3379 P/A/Sgt FRANCIS G.J reported for duty with D/290 Bgde R.F.A to fill vacancy.	UB

WAR DIARY or INTELLIGENCE SUMMARY

Army Form C. 2118.

(54)

Place	Date	Hour	Summary of Events and Information	Remarks and references to Appendices
FOSSEUX	7.8.17		Accompanied A.D.V.S. XVII Corps on inspection of 174 & 175 Infantry Bgde & 214 M.G. Coy	
"	8.8.17		Accompanied A.D.V.S. XVII Corps on inspection of M.V.S., Div Sig Coy R.E. 503, 504, & 511 Coys R.E. Visited LE CROSTISON Farm & there investigated VI Corps Mange Dipping Baths.	
"	9.8.17		Conference of N.O's Present Capts SHEATHER, & GLYNN. Weekly returns forwarded to D.V.S XVII Corps showing Remaining 21 Admitted 36 Total 57 Cured 10 Transferred Sick 12 Died nil Destroyed nil Remaining 35 Total 57. Strength Horses 1246 Mules 477. Total 1723.	
"	10.8.17		SE. 23850 Pt Abrahams A.V.C reported for duty with M.V.S Visited S.S.O with reference to supply of green forage who made arrangements for same	
"	11.8.17		Visited & inspected 2/1 H.C.F.A, 2/4 Lond Regt. 2/2 H.C.F.A, 173 Bgde H.Q, 2/3 Lond Regt 206 M.G. Coy & 510 Coy A.S.C.	
"	13.8.17		Visited & inspected 2/3 H.C.F.A & R.A.H.Q.	
"	14.8.17		Visited & inspected 2/9, 2/10, 2/11 & 2/12 Lond Regts, 215 M.G. Coy, 214 M.G. Coy & 2/5 & 2/6 Lond Regts.	

WAR DIARY
or
INTELLIGENCE SUMMARY

Army Form C. 2118.

Place	Date	Hour	Summary of Events and Information	Remarks and references to Appendices
FOSSEUX	15.8.17		Visited undefeated DHQ, MMR, NVS & 511 Coy A.S.C.	AB
"	16.8.17		Weekly conference of R.O's at this office present Capts SHEATHER & GLYNN. Weekly returns forwarded to A.D.V.S XVII Corps showing. Remaining 35 admitted 30 Total 65. Cured 22 Transport nil. Died 1 Destroyed nil. Remaining 42 Total 65. Strength Horses 1300 Mules 478 Total 1778. Inspected 2/1 & 2/8 Batter & 19.3 M.T. Coy.	JB AB
"	17.8.17		" 503, 509 & 511 Coy RE. Headquarter guard. Horsemastership in 511 Field Coy RE has for some time been bad, today there is much improvement gained lodging letter.	SB
"	19.8.17		Visit to M. MASTISSART, 8 RUE SALTY. BARLY. Examining injured mare advising Area Commandant & Claims Officer with reference to claim by the owner for compensation.	AB
"	21.8.17		Capt. J.G. TAYLOR A.V.O. 1/c 29th Dyn RFA granted 10 days leave in U.K. from today	AB
"	23.8.17		Conference NCO's present Capts SHEATHER & GLYNN. Weekly returns forwarded to A.D.V.S XVII Corps showing. Remaining 42 admitted 42.	AB

WAR DIARY or INTELLIGENCE SUMMARY

Army Form C. 2118.

Place	Date	Hour	Summary of Events and Information	Remarks and references to Appendices
FOSSEUX	23.8.17	a.m.	M.L.O.A. Cured 32 Transpired sick 17 Died 1 Destroyed nil Remaining 34 Total 84. Strength Horses 1296 Mules 438 Total 1734. All animals are in much improved in condition. No onward of the first, orders received for D.H.Q. to move tomorrow - to join XVIII Corps. Fanny	JS/5
YPRES area	24.8.17		D.H.Q. moved to X Camp situated between POPERINGHE & PLANERTINGHE at A.16.c.2.6. Sheet 28 N.W.	JS/6
	25.8.17		Notified A.D.V.S. XVIII Corps of arrival. Situation of Mores. M.V.S. moved from FOSSEUX to (temporary location near POPERINGHE) F.22.C.4.6. Sheet 27.	JS/5
"	26.8.17		Reported personally A.D.V.S. XVIII Corps.	JS/5
"	27.8.17		Inspected all Divisional units in the area.	JS/5
"	28.8.17		Prospecting for suitable site for M.V.S. visited D.A.D.V.S. H.Q.Dr. with reference to taking over units attached to 48th Divn. for VetY Services.	JS/5
"	29.8.17		D.H.Q. moved to camp vacated by 48th Divn. Take over VetY administration of 48th Divisional Artillery (2.A.Bgdes, 241 Bgde R.F.A. + D.A.C.) VetY Officers Capts. V. PRIDE-JONES & J. GREEN. 474, 475 & 477 Coys R.E. & 5th Scout Regt.	

WAR DIARY
or
INTELLIGENCE SUMMARY
(Erase heading not required.)

Army Form C. 2118.

(57)

Place	Date	Hour	Summary of Events and Information	Remarks and references to Appendices
YPRES AREA	29.8.17	Cont'd	The following Other ranks attached to New Div for Vety administration are to New unit :- 102 Bgde R.F.A, 23rd Div Artillery HQ & 109 Coy ASC V.O. i/c Capt D. STARKEY, 103 Bgde R.F.A., V.O. i/c Capt. P.A. CARROL, 126 Army Field Artillery Bgde V.D. i/c Capt M.G. GREEN, 155 Army Field Artillery Bgde V.O. i/c Capt. R.K. PORTEOUS, & 141 Labour Coy. M.V.S. moves to new camp A.28.d.9.4 This is a most excellent camp. for a M.V.S. good Stabling for 90 animals & good accommodation for men, stores, office etc.	93b SQ/5
YPRES Area	30.8.17		Visit M.V.S. & 3/8 Divisional Units	
"	31.8.17		Conference of A.D.Sub this office. Present Capts SHEATHER, GLYNN, PRIDE-JONES, G.GREEN, STARKEY, CARROL & PORTEOUS. Collect & check weekly returns, ascertain location of Officers units, arrange system of evacuation of sick mounted animals, discuss feeding matters.	18/5

N.C.M. Bowden
Major,
D.A.D.V.S.
58th (LONDON) DIVISION.

Army Form C. 2118.

WAR DIARY
or
INTELLIGENCE SUMMARY.

D.A.D.V.S. 58 Div

Vol 9

(Erase heading not required.)

Instructions regarding War Diaries and Intelligence Summaries are contained in F. S. Regs., Part II. and the Staff Manual respectively. Title pages will be prepared in manuscript.

Place	Date	Hour	Summary of Events and Information	Remarks and references to Appendices
YPRES AREA	1-9-17		Attended conference at A.D.V.S. XVIII Corps. Weekly Returns handed in made up as follows. In last Return 207. Admitted 213. Total 414. Evacuated 159. Trans. Sick. 33. Died 14. Destroyed 7. Remaining 198. Total 414. Missing 1. Strength Horses 4633. Mules 1750. Total 6383. Wastage .90%. Daily Casualty Mnre to A.D.V.S. XVIII Corps. Artillery Killed 2. Other Units Killed 8. Wounded 6. Total 16.	JyS
-do-	2-9-17		Inspection of 240 and 241 Base R.F.A, also 48 D.A.C. Visit to A.D.V.S: XVIII Corps with reference to a case of Inspector Sarcy. Capt. J.G. TAYLOR returns to duty after 10 days leave in U.K. Daily casualty Mnre; Artillery wounded 1.	JyS
-do-	3-9-17		Appointment with A.D.V.S. XVIII Corps at 48 D.A.C. Inspect English case of Sarcy. Inspection of animals at 58th Div M.M.S for evacuation. Sergt COTTON A.S.C. 58 M.M.S. Temporarily attached to 174 Inf. Bn, evacuated sick to C.C.S. Daily casualty Mnre "Nil"	JyS
-do-	4-9-17		Inspection of 102 Bde R.F.A + 23rd D.A.C Instructions received from A.D.V.S. XVIII Corps to handset of Capt TAYLOR J.L. to 35. D.I.V. Daily casualty Mnre. Other Units wounded 1.	JyS

T2134. Wt. W708—776. 500000. 4/15. Sir J. C. & S.

Army Form C. 2118.

WAR DIARY
or
INTELLIGENCE SUMMARY.
(Erase heading not required.)

DADVS
58 Div

Place	Date	Hour	Summary of Events and Information	Remarks and references to Appendices
YPRES AREA	5-9-17		Inspection of Animals at Div Train 2/4 Lon Regt. Field Ambulances H.Q. Cy. Co. Visit to M.D. & inspect animals for evacuation. Daily casualty wire. Artillery Kills 6 Wounded 1 Other Units Wounded 2. Total 9.	V.g.S.
do	6.9.17		Inspection of Remounts arriving at RAILHEAD: PROVEN. Daily casualty wire Artillery Wounded 1 Other Units Wounded 3. Total 4.	V.g.S.
do	7-9-17		Conference of V.Os. Present Capts. GLYNN - PRIDE-JONES - STARKEY - GREEN. G. CARROLL. 102 & 103 Bdes RFA, 23rd DAC and 190 Co acc move from 58 Div Area. 290 & 291 Bdes RFA, 58 DAC 509 A.C. arrive in 58 Div Area. Capts TAYLOR & BOYD & RICHMOND report this office with weekly A.2000. Inspection animals at M.D. for evacuation. Capt TAYLOR J.L. RFA leaves to join 35 Div. Daily Casualty Wire Artillery Killed 1 Wounded 6 Other Units Wounded 1.	V.g.S.
do	8.9.17		D.A.D.V.S. attends conference at XVIII Corps, submitting Weekly returns as follows. Sh. East Ret 201 Admitted 2/3. Total 414 Cured 149 Evac. Sick 102 Died 16. Destroy. 4 Remaining 145 Total 414 Strength Horses 4584 Mules 1771. Total 6355 Wastage 1.9 %. Returns for Artillery Sh. East Ret 33 Admitted 39 Total 70 Cures 21 Evans 7 Died 1 Destroy. 2 Remaining 39 Total 70 Strength Horses 1583, Mules 800 Total 2383. Wastage .54%.	V.g.S.

WAR DIARY or INTELLIGENCE SUMMARY

Army Form C. 2118.

Place	Date	Hour	Summary of Events and Information	Remarks and references to Appendices
YPRES AREA.	8.9.17		Obtained assistance of Motor Ambulance to evacuating Horse M.T. Daily Casualty. Mine Artillery Killed 10. Wounded 20. Other Units Killed 3. Wounded 11.	J.S.
-do-	9.9.17		Inspection of 241 Bde R.F.A. & 290, 291 Bde R.F.A. Inspected Animals for evacuation at M.D.T. Daily Casualty Horse Nil.	J.S.
-do-	10.9.17		Inspection of 290 Bde R.F.A. also cases for evacuation M.D.T. RD.V.S. XVIII Corps. Wires to Director Vet. Cavt. & Pr.I.D.F. Jones V.O. & 240 Bde R.F.A. to proceed to 48 Div H.Q. to take up temporary duties as D.A.D.V.S. vice Major Reid who has met with an accident. Daily Casualty Horse Artillery Killed 4. Wounded 7. Other Units Wounded 2.	J.S.
-do-	11.9.17		Visit to 2/3 London Regt. 2/11 Ltn Regt. 2/1 H.C.F.A. Notification received that 14th Corps M.D. closed until Thursday 13th inst. Daily casualty Horse Artillery Killed 6. Wounded 16. Gassed 2. Other Units Gassed 4.	J.S.
-do-	12.9.17		Inspection of 2/9 London Regt. 141 T.M.B. & Animals at M.D.T. for evacuation. Daily Casualty Horse Other Units Wounded 1.	J.S.
-do-	13.9.17		Visit to 48 & 58 Div. Artillery also inspection Animals M.D.T. for evacuation. Daily Casualty Bomb Killed 21. Wounded 66. On Gunshot Wounds Killed 4.	J.S.

WAR DIARY
INTELLIGENCE SUMMARY
(Erase heading not required.)

Army Form C. 2118.

Place	Date	Hour	Summary of Events and Information	Remarks and references to Appendices
YPRES AREA	14.9.17		Conference D.O's present Genls RICHMOND, TAYLOR, GREEN, GLYNN. Inspection of animals at 290 & 291 Bde RFA. Daily Casualty Wire Artillery Bomb. Wounded 3. Gunshot Killed 3. Wounded 3. Total 9.	
do	15.9.17		Conference at H.Q.'s XVIII Corps. Returns submitted were as follows. In Cav Return 129, Admitted 329. Total 458. Cures 87. Evac Sick 63. Died 56. Destroyed 49. Remaining 201. Total 456. Strength three L+56 Mules 189. Total 6293. Wastage 2.6%. Inspection of Animals at M.O.S for evacuation. Daily Casualty Wire Gunshot Killed 1. Artillery	
do	16.9.17		Visit to M.O.S. 2/1, 2/2 & 2/3 I.H.C. 27. Daily Casualty Wire Artillery Gunshot Killed 1. Wounded 1. Other Units Gunshot Killed 5 Wounded 8.	
do	17.9.17		Inspection of Animals M.O.T. for evacuation. Inspecting 4 & L 158 & 2 Div Artillery, investigating increase of OPHTHALMIA cases. Sergt ELLISON M.C. No.70716 reports for duty per no.19 Vety Hospital. Daily Casualty wire - Artillery. Bomb Killed 2. Wounded 5. Gunshot Wounded 3. Other Units Killed 1 Wounded 2.	
do	18.9.17		Inspection of Animals M.V.T. for evacuation. B.ech. 48 D.A.C & 14 L.A.G. Casualty Wire Bomb. Artillery Wounded 1. Gunshot Killed 1 Wounded 1. Other Units. Nil.	

WAR DIARY
INTELLIGENCE SUMMARY

Army Form C. 2118.

Place	Date	Hour	Summary of Events and Information	Remarks and references to Appendices
YPRES AREA	20-9-17		Inspection of Animals at M.O.S. for evacuation. Daily casualty Wire Other Ranks. Killed 5 Wounded 10	V.S.
do	19-9-17		Inspection of 76 Remounts for Div Artillery at PROVEN. TT 0062 P/H/Cpl SPINKS S.S. 58 Div MGT admonies P/H/Sgt. Refs RUC Base Records T.9/60a/17 dates 19-9-17. Daily casualty wire Other Ranks Gunshot killed 5 wounded 10.	V.S.
do	21-9-17		Conference P.O.C present Capts PHEATHER, GLYNN, GREEN RICHMOND, TAYLOR. Inspection of 21 Remounts at PROVEN. Daily casualty Wire Artillery Gunshot Wounded 1 Other Unit Gunshot killed 2.	V.S.
do	22-9-17		Remounts received to A.D.V.S. XVIII Corps by Capt RICHMOND DADVS inspopio in last Return 203, admitted 211, total 414 Evaced 136, Iran over 55, Des 20, destroyed 10 Remaining 203. Total 414 Strength Horses 4401 Mules 2054. Total 6595. Wastage 1.2%. P/A/Sergt ELLIOT E 10.6. Mot Ambulances to No.3 Veterinary Hospital BOULOGNE. Daily casualty Wire - Artillery Killed Gunshot 1 Bomb Killed 1 Wounded 6 Other Units Bomb Killed 12 Wounded 7. Total 27.	V.S.

WAR DIARY
or
INTELLIGENCE SUMMARY.

Army Form C. 2118.

Place	Date	Hour	Summary of Events and Information	Remarks and references to Appendices
YPRES AREA	23-9-17		Inspection of cases at M.O. for evacuation. ADMS XVIII Corps requests the names of NCOs & men recommended for appointments as Sergeants and the following names are submitted. D/A/Cpl A.J. 44711 M. W/S/Cpl CURBISHLEY. P. ROBINSON. E.C. Pte POPE. Daily casualty. Mine artillery. Bombs. Killed 1. Wounded 2. Other Unit: nil	by.
-do-	24-9-17		Daily casualty. Own artillery. Gunshot. Killed 2. Wounded 1. Other Unit: Gunshot. Wounded 2.	by.
-do-	25-9-17		Daily casualty. Mine = Artillery. Gunshot. Killed 1. Wounded 2. Other Unit: nil. Sergt SHARPE G. MC attacks recently sole admitted to Field Amb. Visit to MDS.	by.
-do-	26-9-17		Daily casualty. Mine = Artillery. Bombs. Killed 1. Gunshot. Killed 1. Wounded nil. Other Unit: Gunshot Wounded 2. approval is given by ADMS XVIII Corps to TT0874 V/A/ Lcpl CURBISHLEY. F. to D/A/Cpl.	by.
-do-	27-9-17		Conference of D.O.s Present Capts SHEATHER. TAYLOR. RICHMOND GWYNN. GREEN. SMITH. Weekly return forwarded to ADMS XVIII Corps.	by.

Army Form C. 2118.

WAR DIARY
or
INTELLIGENCE SUMMARY.
(Erase heading not required.)

D.A.D.V.S.
58 Div.

Place	Date	Hour	Summary of Events and Information	Remarks and references to Appendices
YPRES AREA	27-9-17		Made up as follows. In last return 203 Animals 188 Mules 391. Cures 140. Evant with 35. Died 27 Destroyer 2. Remaining 169 Total 391. Strength Horses 4602 Mules 2129. Total 6731 Wastage 9.4%. Daily Casualty Mrs Artillery Gunshot Wounded 2 Other ranks Gunshot Killed 2 Wounded 4. Graves Nil. Capt GREEN G. proceeds on 10 days leave in UK	
-do-	28-9-17		58 D.N.Q. Move to RECQUES ARA, List of Units which came under SP Div Veterinary Administration. handed to D.A.D.V.S. 4th Div together with copies of A 2000 for week ending 27.9.17. A.D.V.S. XIX Corps notified by Wire of arrival, quoting Office Location as BILLET No 2 RUTKEROUL.	H/S N/S
-do-	29-9-17			
-do-	30-9-17		— " —	

WAR DIARY
INTELLIGENCE SUMMARY

Army Form C. 2118.

D.A.D.V.S.
58 Division

Vol. 51 No. 10

Place	Date	Hour	Summary of Events and Information	Remarks and references to Appendices
LUTKERQUE	1/10/17		Inspection of 174 Inf Bde Group. Pte THRESHER. A.V.C. reports for duty from No 2 Vety Hosp. 58 Div MOBS left behind in YPRES AREA in XVIII Corps.	h.S
	2/10/17		Major J SCOTT-BOWDEN. DADVS meets with accident - fracture shoulder and is admitted to No 35 General Hosp CALAIS. Capt M J GLYNN RO to 58 Div TRAIN noted for to carry on duties	h.S
	3/10/17		Capt M J GLYNN AV.C. carries on with duties as D.A.D.V.S	h.S
	4/10/17		Inspection of 173 Inf Bde. Group.	h.S
	5/10/17		Weekly returns sent in to ADVS XIX Corps as follows. In ambulances, In cold Reserve 21 on mules 38 Total 59 Cures 14 Vans 6 Dies 1 Remounts 35 Total 59 Strength Horses 1244 Mules 248 Total 1425 Wastage 4.9%	h.S
	6/10/17		A.D.V.S. XIX Corps visits Office	h.S
			Visits to 2/3 A.C. F.A. 2/9 2/11 2/1 & LONDON REGT. Inspection of 58 Div H.Q.G.	h.S
	7/10/17		Visit to 510 Co A.S.C. 2/2 A.C. F.A.	h.S
	8/10/17		Inspection of 1/4.3 Inf Bde with MOBS XIX Corps	h.S
	9/10/17		Inspection of 1/5 Inf Bde with MOBS XIX Corps.	h (J.C.W ADVS 10/10/17)

WAR DIARY or INTELLIGENCE SUMMARY

Army Form C. 2118.

D.A.D.V.S 56 Division

Page 65

Place	Date	Hour	Summary of Events and Information	Remarks and references to Appendices
DUNKERQUE	10/10/17		Assumed duties of D.A.D.V.S on appointment. Reported arrival to A.D.V.S XIX Corps & 56 Div H.Q.	MB
	11/10/17		Inspected 174 Brigade groups complete also 2/2 H.C.F.A. 2/1 H.C.F.A. 266 M.G.Co. 603 Field Co R.E. 511 Co A.S.C. found animals in good condition & well shod but camping grounds wet & muddy.	MB
	12/10/17		Inspected 56 Div Sig. Co. 2/11 London Regt. Return submitted to A.D.V.S XIX Corps as follows:- For Last Return 35, admitted 21, Total 56, Cured 26, Died 1, Dest. 1, Rem. 28. Total 56 Strength Horses 1241 Mules 440 Total 1681. Wastage .11	MB
	13/10/17		Inspected 510 Co A.S.C. 2/4 London Regt. Eleven men A.V.C. reported from No 24 Vet Hosp. proceeded with 58 Div M.V.S. & stayed the night.	MB
	14/10/17		Eleven men proceeded to M.V.S. situated in Ypres Area. Inspected 174 Brigade complete and A.D.V.S XIX Corps	MB
	15/10/17		Inspected 2/9 2/11 & 2/12 London Regts. 2/14 & 215 M.G. Cos. Received report from A.D.V.S XIX Corps on his inspection of 56 Div Units. Same submitted to Div H.Q. Report was of a very satisfactory nature & stated that animals were in good condition that shoeing was good.	MB
	16/10/17		Inspected & passed for Evacuation nineteen animals, these proceeded direct to No 23 Vet Hosp. St Omer. 17 walking & 2 by Float. Inspected 2/1 2/3 London Regts, 173 B.H.Q. & 56 Div Sigs	MB
	17/10/17		Inspected 2/3 H.C.F.A. This Unit keeps its horses very well & harness also in very good state.	MB

Army Form C. 2118.

D.A.D.V.S.
58 Division.

(6)

WAR DIARY
or
INTELLIGENCE SUMMARY.
(Erase heading not required.)

Place	Date	Hour	Summary of Events and Information	Remarks and references to Appendices
WATROUE	18/10/17		Inspected 175 Brigade group complete. Shoeing very bad, but harness & mules looking wonderfully well	MB
	19/10/17		Weekly Returns submitted G.A.D.V.S. XIX Corps showing. In Last Return 28, Admitted 36, Total 56. Cured 15, Transferred Sick 21, Destroyed 3, Remaining 17. Total 56. Strength Horses 1128 Mules 390	
			Total 1518 Wastage 1.5.	MB
POPERINGHE	20/10/17		D.H.Q. moved from XIX Corps Area (Recques) to Poperinghe joining XVIII Corps. A.D.V.S. XVIII Corps	MB
			XIX Corps hot notified by wire. Took over 58 DIV M.V.S. which had been detached from Div.	MB
	21/10/17		A.D.V.S. XVIII Corps visits office and instructions re Returns	MB
	22/10/17		Inspected 174 Infantry Brigade Complete. Instructions forwarded to Capt Shatter O.C. M.V.S. to	MB
			proceed forthwith on Special Temporary Duty to ABBEVILLE. Daily Casualty Mile NIL	MB
	23/10/17		Inspected 2/5, 2/6, 2/7, 2/8 London Regts 198 M.G.Co. also Inspected 58 DIV M.V.S.	MB
	24/10/17		Visited M.V.S. Capt G.J.B. Sewell reported from No 23 Veterinary Hospital to take over	MB
			temporary Command of M.V.S. during absence of Capt Shatter.	
	25/10/17		D.H.Q. moved to Bucky Camp. Notified A.D.V.S. XVIII Corps of new location.	MB
YPRES AREA	26/10/17		Inspected M.V.S.	MB
	26/10/17		Conference of M.O's at D.A.D.V.S. office present Capts Lyons & Richmond 58 Divisional	
			Artillery required Decision for Veterinary Administration. The following mules were taken over from	

WAR DIARY or INTELLIGENCE SUMMARY

Army Form C. 2118.

(67)

Place	Date	Hour	Summary of Events and Information	Remarks and references to Appendices
YPRES AREA	26/10/17		18 Divisional :- 18 Divisional Artillery Noty Officer Capt. J.S. McCarra & B.J. Bitton. 32 Divisional Artillery Noty Officer Capt. J.S. Hill & J.O. Smith also No 3 Traffic Control by orders.	MVS
			Casualty wise RA GS Killed 9 Wounded 12. Bont Wounded 1 taken Units Bont Killed 1	
	27/10/17		Conference at XVIII Corps A.D.V.S. Office. Weekly Return Submitted by Gilmore. Horse Return 115 Admitted 158 Total 273 Cured 78 Transfered Self 24 Died 22 Destroyed 6 Remain 143 Total 273.	
			Strength Horses 3,593 Mules 1162 Total 3755 Wastage 1.6 Visited M.V.S. Casualty wise RA GS Killed 1.	MVS
	28/10/17		Inspection 58th DAC, DIV Sig R.E., No 3 Traffic Control Squadron. Casualty wise RA GS Killed 7 Wounded 7. Visited MVS.	MVS
	29/10/17		Inspected 32 Div R.A. 320 AC 18st DAC Casualty wise RA GS Killed 12 Wounded 7. Bont Wounded 1 taken Units GS Killed 2.	MVS
	30/10/17		Inspected 3 Troops of K.E.H. & Dept. Right Sections of No 3 Traffic Control Squadron. 58 DAC. 2 men reported for duty at MVS from No 6 Vet. Hosp. Review. Daily Casualties were no longer reported unless Casualties heavy.	MVS
	31/10/17		Inspected 2/1, 2/2 & 2/3 H.C.F.A. & Visited MVS & inspected strayed horses for re-issue. Casualty wise RA GS Killed 6 Wounded 6 Bont Killed 3 Wounded 13.	MVS

M.V. Barron
MAJOR,
D.A.D.V.S.
58th (LONDON) DIVISION.

WAR DIARY
or
INTELLIGENCE SUMMARY.

Army Form C. 2118.

Place	Date	Hour	Summary of Events and Information	Remarks and references to Appendices
YPRES AREA	1/11/17		Visited & Inspected 3/15 M.G.Co also 2/9, 2/10, 2/11 & 2/12 Battalions London Regiments 175 Brigade H.Q. & 174 Brigade Groups Bombs.	MLB
	2/11/17		Visited ADVS at II Corps H.Q. Returns submitted G.ADVS II Corps as follows: For Last Return 260 admitted 521 Total 781 Cured 199 Destroyed Sick 85 Died 89 Discharged 64 Remaining 344 Total 781. Strength Horses 5889 Mules 2711 Total 8600. Wastage 2.7	MLB
	3/11/17		Visited Mobile Veterinary Section. Office Work	MLB
	4/11/17		Conference at II Corps H.Q. with ADVS. Visited M.V.S.	MLB
	5/11/17		Visited Divisional Artillery at Reninge Area	MLB
	6/11/17		Visited Corps H.Q. ADVS at 9am, rode to Peselhoek & arranged for horses & returns for exam. hasty. Visited M.V.S. & examined all animals for Evacuation.	MLB
	7/11/17		9.30 to 6.30pm at Peselhoek superintending evacuation of horses by train from 3 Aust.V.H.S. Visited M.V.S.	MLB
	8/11/17		Visited 174 & 175 Brigade Groups Complete	MLB
	9/11/17		Conference of MOs at my Office. Return. Visited ADVS II Corps & went to Peselhoek re train M.L.B.	MLB
	10/11/17		Visited Divisional Advanced H.Q. also ADVS II Corps. Submitted returns G.ADVS II Corps as follows: For last Return 342 Admitted 359 Total 701 Cured 195 Transferred Sick 117 Died 13	MLB

WAR DIARY
or
INTELLIGENCE SUMMARY.
(Erase heading not required.)

Army Form C. 2118.

Place	Date	Hour	Summary of Events and Information	Remarks and references to Appendices
YPRES AREA	10/11/17		Destroyed 14 Remaining 359 Total 701 Strength Horses 577/2 Mules 2725 Total 6497 Wastage .39	MCB
	11/11/17		Visited Public & examined all animals for evacuation next day	MCB
	12/11/17		all day entraining at Peselhoek	MCB
	13/11/17		Visited 32nd Divisional Artillery + M.V.S.	MCB
	14/11/17		Visited 16th Divisional Artillery + own M.V.S.	MCB
	15/11/17		Visited 174 + 175 Brigade Groups Canfield + M.V.S	MCB
	16/11/17		Conferency C.O's in my office. Return Mules & Horses Centres Expediture + R.E.H	MCB
			Submitted Return G.A.D.V.S II Corps Remaining 267 Admitted Horses 185 Total 442 Cured 141	MCB
			Transferred Sick 75 Died 16 Destroyed 5 Remaining 205 Total 442 Strength of Horses 4297 Mules 1955	MCB
			Was 615 = 3 Wastage 1.4	MCB
PROVEN	17/11/17		Office removed from BORDER CAMP to PROVEN	MCB
	18/11/17		Visited Mobile Veterinary Section, Divisional Signals + H.Q. Horses. East Office went to	MCB
			Englouder 15 days leave.	MCB
	19/11/17		Visited M.V.S. office MCB	MCB
	20/11/17		" Inspected 175 Brigade HQ 511 Coy R.E. 2/9 + 2/10 Londons Regt + 2/3 HC 39	MCB
	21/11/17		" 2/10 + 2/11 London Regt	MCB

Army Form C. 2118.

WAR DIARY
or
INTELLIGENCE SUMMARY.
(Erase heading not required.)

Instructions regarding War Diaries and Intelligence Summaries are contained in F. S. Regs., Part II. and the Staff Manual respectively. Title pages will be prepared in manuscript.

Place	Date	Hour	Summary of Events and Information	Remarks and references to Appendices
PROVEN	22/11/17		Returns. Visited N.V.S. & 175 Brigade Group.	
	23/11/17		Visited M.V.S. & inspected 173 Brigade Group Complete. Div Signals & M.B. Submitted returns to A.D.V.S XIX Corps. Remaining 18 admitted Sick 36 Total 54 Cured 14 Transferred Sick & Died 1 Discharged 2 Remaining 29	MCB
			Total 54 Strength Horses 1192 Mules 410 Total 1602 Wastage 62 (18 4:1:32 Div Artillery was horsed from 6 other respective Divisions) Submitted returns of 58 Div Artillery to A.D.V.S XVIII Corps - to follows Remaining 122	
			Return & last return 99 Admitted 184 Total 183 Cured 50 Transferred Sick 10 Died 1 Remaining 122	
			Total 183 Strength Horses 1457 Mules 771 Total 2228 Wastage 59.	MCB
	24/11/17		Visited 174 Brigade Group & M.V.S.	MCB
	25/11/17		Visited M.V.S. Capt Hardie returned from leave. A.D.V.S XIX Corps visited M.V.S. Evacuated horses for evacuation to C.C.C.S.	MCB
NEILLE	26/11/17		Moved G NIELLE & reported arrival to A.D.V.S XVIII Corps	MCB
	27/11/17		Inspected 175 Brigade & saw to M.V.S. arrival & getting proper accommodation.	MCB
	28/11/17		Visited M.V.B. & was visited by A.D.V.S XVIII Corps.	MCB
	29/11/17		Visit from A.D.V.S XVIII Corps & visited M.V.S.	MCB
	30/11/17		Office Work. Submitted returns (minus Artillery) to A.D.V.S XVIII Corps. - Remaining 27 Total 47 Strength Horses 1310 Mules 418 Total 1728 Wastage 5.	MCB
			Total 47 Cured 19 Transferred Sick 1 Remaining 27 Total 47 Strength Horses 1310 Mules 418 Total 1728 Wastage 5. MCBarron A.D.V.S. 58th (LONDON) DIVISION.	MCB

WAR DIARY or INTELLIGENCE SUMMARY
Army Form C. 2118.

DAD VS
52 Division
71

Place	Date	Hour	Summary of Events and Information	Remarks and references to Appendices
NIELLE	1/12/17		Visited & Inspected in Stables Area B + C Batteries also A + C Batteries	MKB
			of 290 B,10,70 + B Echelon D.A.C. r also 519 Co A.S.C.	MKB
	2/12/17		Visited Mobile Veterinary Section + inspected 175 B. H.Q. + Group	MKB
	3/12/17		"	MKB
	4/12/17		Inspected D.H.Q. + Div Signals	MKB
	5/12/17		174 B. Groups also 510 + 511 Coy A.S.C.	MKB
	6/12/17		175 B " Capt Richmond OBVC 291 B RCA	MKB
			Proceeded 14 days leave to U.K.	MKB
	6/12/17		Visited M.V.S. 510 Coy A.S.C. + 213 H.C. + Conf	MKB
	7/12/17		Conference of MO's at DADVS Office. Nightly Returns submitted to Corps. as follows	MKB
			K. Cot. Return 124 admitted 37 Total 161 Cured 70 Transferred sick 19 Destroyed 1 Remaining 71	
			Lot 161 Strength Horses 2,679 mules 1175 Total 3854 Wastage .5 1	MKB
YPRES AREA	8/12/17		D.H.Q. moved to YPRES AREA. Office established at Welsh Farm	MKB
	9/12/17		Reported arrival to ADVS II Corps. Inspected 290 B,10,70	MKB
	10/12/17		Ypres Work. Inspected D.A.C.	MKB
	11/12/17		Visited ADVS II Corps + M.V.S.	MKB
	12/12/17		Inspected 2/8, 4/3, 2/9, 2/10, 2/11 + 2/12 Battalions	MKB

DADVS
56 Division
Army Form C. 2118.

WAR DIARY
or
INTELLIGENCE SUMMARY.   72

(Erase heading not required.)

Place	Date	Hour	Summary of Events and Information	Remarks and references to Appendices
YPRES AREA	13/12/17		Inspected 214 & 215 Div. G. Coy. 174 B. + O. 9/8 L. Batt. 176 8 H.S. 2/9 2/10 2/11 & 2/12 Batt.	MCB
	14/12/17		Conference of V.Os at D.A.D.V.S. Office. Mob. Return submitted to ADVS II Corps as follows-	MCB
			No. East. Return 71. Admitted 111. Total 182. Cured 33. Inoperables 23. Died 5. Destroyed 2. Remaining 120.	
			Sick 182. Strength Horses 2715. Mules 1246. Total 3961. Wastage 721.	MCB
	15/12/17		Conference at ADVS Office II Corps H.Q. Visited M.V.S.	MCB
	16/12/17		Inspected 173 B. Groups.	MCB
	17/12/17		at Penthoek entraining 127 animals. Visited M.V.S.	MCB
	18/12/17		Inspected 174 & 175 B. Groups.	MCB
	19/12/17		Inspected 58 DAC. Visited M.V.S.	MCB
	20/12/17		Inspected 2/9/1 B. & OC.	MCB
	21/12/17		Conference of VOs at DADVS Office. Mob. Return submitted to ADVS II Corps as	
			follows. No East. Return 120. Admitted 54. Total 174. Cured 77. Inoperables 40. Died 3.	
			Destroyed 2. Remaining 52. Total 174. Strength Horses 2675. Mules 1238. Total 3913. Wastage 71.	MCB
	31/12/17		Proceeded on 14 days Leave to England. ADVS II Corps notified. Duties of DADVS	
			carried on by Capt. Heather OC 2/1 Lond VS. Capt. Richmond returned from 14	
			days leave 21/12/17.	MCB

WAR DIARY
or
INTELLIGENCE SUMMARY.

Army Form C. 2118.

D.A.D.V.S. 58 Div

Place	Date	Hour	Summary of Events and Information	Remarks and references to Appendices
YPRES AREA	23/12/17		Office duties	
	24/12/17		do. Notification received that Sergt CORLYN E07 to C N°22 was killed by Bomb dropped from hostile aircraft and a reference in reply from End.	
	25/12/17		Office duties. Instructions received from A.D.V.S. Corps, re return of AT A20010 due to Knee wound received in Horse M.O. commencing Dec 28th H	
	26/12/17		Office duties	
	27/12/17		do. D.A/ Capt McCALLAN Tr. A.V.C. 77082 reports to duty. Visit D Battery 300 Bn R.F.A. v.c. 2A/Sgt FRANCIS 12327.9	
	28/12/17		Monthly returns on duties to H.Q.1 S.I. Ind Corp. Made up as follows. On that return 52 Admitted 60 Total 152 Cured 40 Transferred 40 Died 3 Destroyed 1 Remaining 68 Total 152 Strength Horses 27/35 Mules 1330 Total 3065.	
	29/12/17		Visit to 171 Division 1. on 86.	
	30/12/17		Office duties. TT91.5 watch R2B Nov E.V.C. parts the to 2NCha 8 Air Ref Smith's See Evidence	
	31/12/17		Office duties	

A. Swinton Capt Major,
A/ D.A.D.V.S.

WAR DIARY
or
INTELLIGENCE SUMMARY.
(Erase heading not required.)

Army Form C. 2118.

Place	Date	Hour	Summary of Events and Information	Remarks and references to Appendices
ELVERDINGHE	1/11/18		Office duties.	
do	2/11/18		Office duties. Inspection of S.A.O. horses	
do	3/11/18		Office duties	
do	4/11/18		Further returns sent in to ADVS. Tn° Bds as follows:– Strand – On last return 49. Admits 89. Trs & 138. Evac. 21. Evac to air 66. Died 1. Remaining 16. Sk 16. 132. Shingk 266. Tres/Am 2.5%. Notions 2. Remaining 16. Sk 16. 2nd Tn 3 Cured. Evac to Sk 16. Diate S.– On last return 19. Admits 24. Trs & 43. Shingk 1245. Nrchi 1.2%.	
do	5/11/18		Returns sent in 19. Sk 16 43. Shingk 1245. Nrchi 1.2%.	
do	6/11/18		Office duties	
do	"		do. C.P.2355. Private BARRETT. P. the re 800 B. on duty with C.220 Bn R.F.	
do	7/11/18		do	
do	8/11/18		do	

CW Sheather Capt
for
Major,
A.D.V.S.
58th (LONDON) DIVISION.

WAR DIARY
or
INTELLIGENCE SUMMARY

Army Form C. 2118.

(75)
S.A.A. 51 Division

Place	Date	Hour	Summary of Events and Information	Remarks and references to Appendices
COUTHOVE	JAN 9		D.H.Q. DAC & COUTHOVE	
		10	Officer Patrol arising returns to certain patrols in the area	M.D.
		11	Posted 4 Rk. & G.S. 173 Bde Group, Infantry returning to trenches	
			A.Coy 76, E.ADYS II Coy 6 Officers – H.M.G. Posts Return 36 Officers 108	
			Sept 156 O.R. & 146 serviceable 3 Coy 3 O.R.s W.S. Sept 156	
			Men R 595 Musketry 66" Rates & Hd Return 14 Over Posts H.E. 37	
			Covert Traps 24 Overboots B 4 hb Ceils 37 Mrs 11 & 57 Water 98°	M.D.
		12	Posted & Hy G. 176 & 130 Bde & Gp Com Posts	M.D.
		13	175	M.D.
		14	Div Artillery H.Q. A.D., Bay S.A.B.S. & 410 S. S.O.S.-A.B.	
			Cdr. H.A.O.C. instructed to have sent Remounts & hay 14 of By R.H.A Lt & 3rd	M.D.
			Returns sub over due Div Sign + Infantry Brigades	M.D.
		15	Another Gunner & Officer	M.D.
		16	D.V.S. D.A.H. DAC	M.D.
		17	Coy D RE Coy	M.D.
		18	Another Gunner Officer Return & D.V.S II Coy & D.Y.S II Coy 3rd Infantry	M.D.

Army Form C. 2118.

WAR DIARY
or
INTELLIGENCE SUMMARY.
(Erase heading not required.)

76

Place	Date	Hour	Summary of Events and Information	Remarks and references to Appendices
OUTHOVE			Honours to List (return) 82 Admitted 61 Total 143 Cured 44 Transferred 52 Remaining 47)	
			total 143 Stamped 2567 Wastage 19% Mules to East Ret. 16 admitted 19 Total 35 Cured 15	mb
			Horses & Rem. 13 total 35 Stamped 1094 Wastage 56%.	
	JAN 19		Office Routine	mb
	20		D.H.Q. leave II Corps Area to join III Corps.	mb
CORBIE	21		Intimation of arrival sent to III Corps.	mb
	22		M.I.S arrived. Visited & Inspected DIV Signals, 513 Coy ASC, 503 & 504 Coy RE	mb
	23		Inspected DAC & MVS	mb
	24		Visited MVS. Office Routine	mb
	25		Conference at Office. Return Submitted GADYS III Corps as follows:—	mb
			Horses & East Return 47 Admitted 69 Total 116 Cured 35 Trans 18 Died 1 Des 6 Rem 66	
			Total 116 Stamped 2546 Wastage 97%. Mules N.&E. Ret. 13 Admitted 9 Total 22 Cured 12	
			Trans. 2 Rem. 5 Total 22 Stamped 1229 Wastage nil	
	26		Visited NWS + 173 O H.Q.	mb
	27		" " + 509 Coy ASC	mb
	28		Office Routine. Submitted Nominal Roll of all Officers, NCO's & Men	mb

DADVS 58
Army Form C. 2118.
Vol 13

WAR DIARY
or
INTELLIGENCE SUMMARY.
(Erase heading not required.)

Place	Date	Hour	Summary of Events and Information	Remarks and references to Appendices
CORBIE	JAN 29		Office routine	
	30		Visited & Inspected 173 & 175 Brigade Groups Complete	
	31		Visited New Area for Inspection for site for M.V.S.	

M Barron Major A.V.C.
DADVS 58 Division

Army Form C. 2118.

WAR DIARY
INTELLIGENCE SUMMARY.
S.S. of 58 Division

Vol 14

(Erase heading not required.)

Instructions regarding War Diaries and Intelligence Summaries are contained in F. S. Regs., Part II. and the Staff Manual respectively. Title pages will be prepared in manuscript.

Place	Date	Hour	Summary of Events and Information	Remarks and references to Appendices
CORBIE	28/2/18		Inspected 58 Div Signal Co. and W.V.C. Weekly returns submitted to 15 Corps. 3 Rops. applied for. Force on Instruction 5a O division 53 total 109. Division 36 Officers refused 10 Sergeants 2 Privates. Maintenance 50 total 10 L. Division 2508 Frontage 4389.	
			Men on Instruction & Division M. 22 Ofcs C 30 Que M 8 Other rk 6	
			4 Remaining under treatment 18. B 30 Other rk 1224	
do	2/3/18		Marches. 33.90	CyS
do	3/3/18		Inspected 291 Brigade R.F.A.	CyS
do	4/3/18		Office routine.	CyS
do	5/3/18		Conference at HQ 2nd Corps and inspecting new site. Major M.K. Barrow. AMC. A.D.M.S. succeeded to new Stationery Hospital East C.B. Clarke. M.C. O.C. 58 Div M.I. who goes Temporary duty to A.D.M.S.	CyS
do	6/3/18		Office duties.	CyS
do	7/3/18		N.V. move by road to BOUCHOIR en route to new area, staying behind to deal with correspondence and returns.	CyS

WAR DIARY or INTELLIGENCE SUMMARY

Army Form C. 2118.

(79)

Place	Date	Hour	Summary of Events and Information	Remarks and references to Appendices
CORBIE	9/2/18		Returns submitted to HQ AVC 3rd Corps made up as follows:—	
			HORSES On last return 50 admitted 6x 06 Cas 223 Issued 26 Evacuated 13 Destroyed. Remaining 62 Est. 20 Strength 12.	
			MULES On last return 6 transferred. 2516 Wastage. 50% Total 26. Issued 14 Remaining under treatment Feb 9 26. Strength 13M Tractor M.L. 18.23M 2nd Line 20 = 860M 3rd Line R.F.A.	
			reports on duty work C2 Hvy Bde R.F.A.	CYB
			Standing office moves from C2 R3 IE and is established at	CY8
DAMPCOURT	10/2/18		DAMPCOURT.	
do			Inspection of 201 Bde R.F.A. and 87 Cav Bde & Corps Cavalry Inspected in C Battery 201 Bde R.F.A. Animals dragged main lines carefully out and all necessary measures taken.	CYB
do	11/2/18		Part of 51 Co. half animals together with stallion mule continued	CYB
do	12/2/18		Veterinary charge taken over of HQ & Army G.S. R.F.A. during its absence of C.M. Hunter AVC on leave.	
			had to start 36cabs, and inspection of Hvy G 201 Bde R.F.A. also inspected 340 Bde R.F.A.	CYB

Army Form C. 2118.

WAR DIARY
or
INTELLIGENCE SUMMARY.
(Erase heading not required.)

31.2.18 58 Div

Place	Date	Hour	Summary of Events and Information	Remarks and references to Appendices
DAMPCOURT	13/2/18		Mobile vertue and Other duties	CRAB
do	14/2/18		do animals fully with baltery	CRAB
do	15/2/18		Inspection of 58th D.A.C. Weekly returns submitted. A.D.V.S 3 Corps watched 4 horses on last return admitted 5. 13. Total 140. Cured 36. Transferred 17. Destroyed 2. Remaining main treatment 85. Total 140. Strength 3063. Wastage 6190. Mules. In last return 11. Admitted 22. Total 33. Cured 4. Transferred 6. Sationary 1. Remaining under treatment 19. Total 33. Strength 1412. Wastage 4%	
do	16/2/18		Office duties and MvS routine	CRAB
do	17/2/18		Inspection of 2/B A.B.Ja 402 Battery RHA O & Z Batteries R.H.A. 365 Forestry Co. Worked sawing wood 7 G 145 Inf. Bde. 215 Infy Coy 503 R.E.	CRAB
do	18/2/18		Inspection of proposed new stables to be allotted to 2/10 Lond RFA. situated the CHARNY - VILLEQUIER ROAD	CRAB
do	19/2/18		Other duties and MvS routine.	CRAB

WAR DIARY
INTELLIGENCE SUMMARY

Army Form C. 2118.

Place	Date	Hour	Summary of Events and Information	Remarks and references to Appendices
DAMPCOURT	20/2/18		Inspection of 201 Bn R.F., 50 Fd R.E. & East Surreys. No Inf Bde	
do	21/2/18		2nd W.L. Coy, 503 Coy A.S.C. 2/1 H.G.Y.A. Senior conference A.D.V.S. 3 Corps also	
do	22/2/18		J.C.M. for trial of the Yellow D Kits Inspection 58 Inf Bde and 51 Coy rob weekly returns submitted to A.D.V.S. 3 Corps No following horses on evacuation 85 Mules. Total No. tourch No. 140 Sick & Lonsking 36 sick horses. 2 Remaining under treatment 109 Total No. struck off 299. Meeting A.D.V.S. with Stallions	
do	23/2/18		Turnd of Sergeant Braun ill with Stallions with Stallions	
do	24/2/18		Office routine MVS 200 ton	
do	25/2/18		Inspected Ho 3 Battery R.N.W. R.F.A. Ays 5 Army & H.Q.V. 3 Corps.	
do	26/2/18		Office duties examination of Journals at H.Q.	
do	27/2/18		Office routine	
do	28/2/18		Conference D.D.V.S. at A.A. & Q.M.G. Office W.O.E routine	

C.H. Shealton Lt Col
A.D.V.S. 58th (LONDON) DIVISION

Army Form C. 2118.

WAR DIARY
or
INTELLIGENCE SUMMARY.
(Erase heading not required.)

D.A.D.V.S.
58 Dn.

Instructions regarding War Diaries and Intelligence Summaries are contained in F. S. Regs., Part II. and the Staff Manual respectively. Title pages will be prepared in manuscript.

[Stamp: 58th (LONDON) DIVISION ✱ VETERINARY ✱ Date 31/3/18]

Place	Date	Hour	Summary of Events and Information	Remarks and references to Appendices
HAMPCOURT	1/3/18		Weekly returns submitted to A.D.V.S. III Corps. as follows. HORSES - Inspection 102 Admitted	
			40 Total 142 Cured 50 Trans 26 Destroyes 1 Remaining 65 Total 142	
			Strength 2893 Wastage .02% MULES. In last return 16 Admitted 12 Total	
			28 Cured 10 Trans 3 Remaining 15 Total 28 Strength 1392 Wastage .23%	
			Inspection of D.A.D.V.S. horses	C&S
"	2/3/18		Office duties and Mobile Routine	C&S
"	3/3/18		Inspection of 403 Batty R.M.A. 1V4dvt Bde H.Q. C/291 Bde R.F.A. 82 S.Q.	C&S
"	4/3/18		Office duties + Mobile Routine	C&S
"	5/3/18		do. Inspected 51 Coy do 2/3 M6 S.A.	C&S
"	6/3/18		Visited A.D.V.S. corps. M.T. Routine	
"	7/3/18		Conference of A.D.V.S. Office. Inspection of 2/3 M6 S.A. 51 Co. A.S.C.	C&S
			M.T. Routine preparing to evacuation sick horses	
"	8/3/18		Weekly returns submitted to A.D.V.S. III Corps as follows Horses last Return 95	
			Admitted 59 Total 154 Cured 52 Trans 14 Transf. to other formations 2 Dies 1	
			Destroyes 1 Remaining 84 Total 154 Strength 2814 Wastage .56%	
			MULES In last Return 15 Admitted 14 Total 29 Cured 10 Trans 1 Destroyed	C&S
			Remaining 14 Total 29 Strength 1253 Wastage .15%	

Army Form C. 2118.

WAR DIARY
or
INTELLIGENCE SUMMARY. VETERINARY.

(Erase heading not required.)

Instructions regarding War Diaries and Intelligence Summaries are contained in F.S. Regs., Part II. and the Staff Manual respectively. Title pages will be prepared in manuscript.

Place	Date	Hour	Summary of Events and Information	Remarks and references to Appendices
DAMPCOURT.	8/3/18		Capt TAYLOR J.G. A.V.C. Granted 14 days leave in UK Nov 8th S 22nd	CX/5
"	9/3/18		Inspected A.V.6 loan Rly Ypo. 512 H.Q. Co.	
"	9/3/18		M.V.S. Routine. Inspects 40 horses.	CX/5
"	10/3/18		Inspected 2/3 H6 FA Misc Office duties	CX/5
"	11/3/18		2 cases of EPIZOOTIC LYMPHANGITIS in C/291 Bde RFA. Animals destroyed	CX/5
"			and all necessary precaution taken	
"	12/3/18		Inspects C Battery 291 Bde R.F.A. No 2 Sect D.A.C	CX/5
"	13/3/18		A.D.V.S. 3 Corps inspects M.V.S. Also inspects C Batty 291 Bde R.F.A.	CX/5
"			Major J. SCOTT BOWDEN arrives to take over duties as A.D.V.S	

A.H. Sheather Capt AVC
A.D.V.S.
58 London Division

Army Form C. 2118.

WAR DIARY
or
INTELLIGENCE SUMMARY

(Erase heading not required.)

58th (LONDON) DIVISION 83

Place	Date	Hour	Summary of Events and Information	Remarks and references to Appendices
QUIERZY	13/3/18		Arrived at 58th Div. Headquarters on appointment DADVS. Authority DVS. RO 387d/1-3-18. Reported to AD. LADVS III Corps at VENIZEL-SUR-AISNE.	ADVS
do	14/3/18		Conference of MOs. Present Capt. SHEATHER, RICHMOND, & GLYNN. Re-arrangement of Veterinary Charges into areas. Inspection of 291 Bgde. RFA & MVS.	ADVS
do	15/3/18		Weekly returns forwarded to ADVS III Corps. Showing Horses & Mules Return R4 admitted 70 Total 154. Cured 53. Transferred Sick 14. Died 2. Destroyed 4. Remaining 81. Total 154. Strength 2874. Wastage 6.9%. Mules Evac. Return 17. Admitted 6. Total 23. Cured 16. Trans Sick 2. Rem. 5. Wd. 0.23. Strength 1292. Wastage .07%.	ADVS
do	16/3/18		Inspected DHQ Group 41 + C Field Amb. 511 Coy. ASC Trks. Conference at ADVS's Office III Corps. In-istep of Lt Col Butty. 290 Bgde RFA. Found mange require re-examination 10 cases EMS. Inspected 16th Entrenching Bat" attached.	ADVS ADVS
do	17/3/18		509 FFO Corps ASC, DHQ Group, Y MVS, Case of Shipolin.	ADVS
do	18/3/18		Lymphangitis reported from C/291 Bgde RFA confirmed by microscope solution Case referred to ADVS III Corps. Most always holding isolation & all precautions	ADVS

Army Form C. 2118.

WAR DIARY
or
INTELLIGENCE SUMMARY
(Erase heading not required.)

Instructions regarding War Diaries and Intelligence Summaries are contained in F. S. Regs., Part II. and the Staff Manual respectively. Title pages will be prepared in manuscript.

Place	Date	Hour	Summary of Events and Information	Remarks and references to Appendices
QUERRIEU	18/3/18		Cont'd. Precautions taken to record being taken in unit of all remarks of injuries.	SLS
do	19/3/18		Inspection of 291 Bde RFA & 171 Sqd Bde. Special care being taken not to C/291 all clothing had fine wearers Boards hanging to side of E.C. animals being destroyed found evacuated to unit etc. all animals chargeon unit carefully examined but no further evidence of Biyastic Lymphangitis observed. A.E.C animals evacuated to M.V.S.	SLS
			Instructions received from ADVS M.O to talk over very admirable of 96 AFA & 291 Bde. This unit straight out from England, all animals to be kneeled as early as possible.	SLS
do	20/3/18		Inspected 404, 405 Batteries 96 AFA at MARICOURT. Vets not yet arrived found majority of horses newly clipped, animals looking very turned up & feeling effects very much. Several fever cases. G.O.C 3rd Div. inspected M.V.S. & AFA expressing satisfaction at the smartness & cleanliness of the unit. G.O.C Maj Gen A.B.E CATOR DSO.	SLS
do	21/3/18		Inspected unit case for preservation at M.V.S. & BAC 96 AFA at MARIES?	SLS

Army Form C. 2118.

WAR DIARY
or
INTELLIGENCE SUMMARY.
(Erase heading not required.)

Place	Date	Hour	Summary of Events and Information	Remarks and references to Appendices
QUIERZY.	21/3/18	Cont'd	Conference M.O.s who received their unit relieve travel instructions regarding evacuation of Sick & Attaluire cases. Several being utilised in the units during my inspections	SH
do	22/3/18		Capt. C.H. SHEATHER P.O. M/S proceeded on leave to England 23 3/18 6.4.18 Weekly returns forwarded to VII Corps showing Horses Str. 82 Admit: 66 Total 148. Curch 41. Trans Sick 45. Destroy 2 Rem. 60. Total 148. Strength 2841. Mule Tars 1.690. Mules Cav. Rt. 8. April 10 Total 18. Curch 2 Trans Sick A. Died 1 Destroy 1 Rem 7 Total 18. Strength 1282 Mule Tars 247.90. Moved to BRETIGNY & VII Corps billeted. DUO inspected Greece. Capt. SHEATHER.	SH SH
BRETIGNY.	23/3/18		Instructions from DDO to move M/S from QUIERCOURT to MORLINCOURT. the former village having been evacuated. Staff Sergt ALDEN & personel of M/S despatched 9 by 6.30am following morning had all front cases moved trans-side which shed previously selected arranged.	AB
do	24/3/18		Office moves to CAMELIN. Visit M/S at MORLINCOURT were orders to Stand by & be ready to move at a moment's notice theling all believe Cont'd	SH

WAR DIARY
INTELLIGENCE SUMMARY

Army Form C. 2118.

Place	Date	Hour	Summary of Events and Information	Remarks and references to Appendices
BRETIGNY	24/3/18		[illegible] marched towards before leaving. No enemy here [illegibly] advancing towards the village. Section two civilians returned to B.H.Q. einhen the same, but instructed to await H.Q. orders before moving.	
CAMELIN	25/3/18		Received orders from D.H.Q. to move M.V.S. at once to CARLEPONT via VARESNES. Failing that route to RIBECOURT via NOYON. On despatch immediately but as enemy guns had destroyed bridge over OISE canal impossible to reach CARLEPONT. NOYON was then being shelled but went on through RIBECOURT without casualties. Bivouaced there overnight. Scores had the stuff but remember of Evacuation cases here only entrained at NOYON for ? Hospital. Heavy M.V. stores had to be abandoned at MARLINCOURT but there were all destroyed before leaving. Office moved to NAMPCEL.	ЗЯ8
NAMPCEL	26/3/18		M.V.S moves from RIBECOURT to CARLEPONT. This place is unsuitable being surrounded by heavy artillery, decide to move on to NAMPCEL afternoon.	ЗЯ8
do	27.3.18		Find urgent accommodation for personnel. M.V.S. inspected. Dir Farrier	ЗЯ8

Army Form C. 2118.

WAR DIARY
or
INTELLIGENCE SUMMARY.
(Erase heading not required.)

Instructions regarding War Diaries and Intelligence Summaries are contained in F. S. Regs., Part II. and the Staff Manual respectively. Title pages will be prepared in manuscript.

Place	Date	Hour	Summary of Events and Information	Remarks and references to Appendices
NAMPCEL	27.3.18	Cont	Any Horse Transport, R.A details & H.Q units	SLB
do	28.3.18		Conference of V.O's present Capt. RICHMOND & GLYNN who report being in touch with all units under their charge. Weekly reports.	SLB
do	29.3.18		Weekly Returns submitted showing Horses Load Rat 60 Admit 73 Total 133. Cured 30 Trans Sick 22 Died 41 Destroy 2 Rem 38. Total 133 Strength 2634 Wastage 10. Mustage 2.7 %. Mules Load Rat 7 Admit 6 Total 13 Cured 3 Died 3 Destroy 2 Rem 5 Total 13 Strength 1222 Wastage 40%. Capt J.E. TAYLOR M.O. Vet. returned from leave. Leave expired 22.3.18 9.00 for Capt. SHEATHER has not been able to inform. Ammunition Report for week forwarded to A.D.V.S. Tele copy reply to D.H.Q. Office moved to AUDIGNICOURT.	SLB
AUDIGNICOURT	30/3/18		Met Capt R.F. STIRLING and V.M.C. 96 A.F.A. Bgde the reports being out of touch with his Batteries Replied to be moving next with his Bgde Headquarter to reform new Brigade 7A. As the Division 58" to 2 V.O. short, I decided after consultation with "Q" 16 Div & O.C. 96 A.F.A. 13 to retain Capt STIRLING at Wash him temporary with as O.C. 68 Div M.V.S. I was unable to	SLB

Army Form C. 2118.

WAR DIARY
or
INTELLIGENCE SUMMARY

(Erase heading not required.)

Instructions regarding War Diaries and Intelligence Summaries are contained in F. S. Regs., Part II. and the Staff Manual respectively. Title pages will be prepared in manuscript.

Place	Date	Hour	Summary of Events and Information	Remarks and references to Appendices
AUDIENCOURT	30.3.18		Could communicate with either III Corps or 4 Army for advice or instructions by telephone.	
			On this matter, but reported my actions by D.R.L.S. to 58' D.H.Q. & A.D.V.S. III Corps.	DRS
do	31.3.18		Visit M.V.S. find Capt. STIRLING has assumed command involved	ADS
			that cases for evacuation may be sent to LA MALADRERIE RETHONDES	
			This appeared in Ordre General d'Evacuation of the 1er Corps de Cavalerie	
			dated 26.3.18 but up to the present there has not been received	ADS
			to forward any cases.	
			Date of Embarkation 19.1.1917	

[signature]
Major,
D.A.D.V.S.
58th (LONDON) DIVISION.

WAR DIARY
or
INTELLIGENCE SUMMARY.

(Erase heading not required.)

Army Form C. 2118.

Instructions regarding War Diaries and Intelligence Summaries are contained in F.S. Regs., Part II. and the Staff Manual respectively. Title pages will be prepared in manuscript.

Place	Date	Hour	Summary of Events and Information	Remarks and references to Appendices
AUDIGNICOURT	1/4/18		Inspected animals at M.V.S. for evacuation. War Diary for month of March forwarded to H.Q.	SM3
CHEVILLECOURT	2/4/18		Nine mares to CHEVILLECOURT. Inspect animals of Divisional Train, 12 animals evacuated by M.V.S. into French Veterinary Hospital at AMBLENY.	SM3
do	3/4/18		Inspect animals of 5"B" DAC, 96th BAC & 59th Artillery Details. One riding horse belonging to 504 Coy R.E. left with No. LEMOINE, CHEVILLECOURT, & Horse Recovery from No. 1 Served.	SM3
CUTRY	4/4/18		Move to CUTRY. Instructions issued to M.V.S. to move to ST. PIERRE-EIGLE. Inspect Sn. Field Ambulance & 174 Inf/14 Bde. Collection greatly interior.	SM3
VILLERS-COTTERETS	5/4/18		Move to VILLERS-COTTERETS to entrain.	SM3
SALEUX	6/4/18		Detrain at LONGUEAUX & move to SALEUX. ADVS III notified arrival. Return forwarded to III Corps showing Horses Lost/Ret 38, Admit 53, Total 91, Cured 32, Trans Sick 9, Died 3, Destroy 1, Rem 46, Total 91, Strength 2021, Wastage 4.9%. Mules Lost/Ret 5, Admit 10, Total 15, Cured 5, Trans Sick 3, Died 4, Rem 3, Total 15, Strength 12/15, Wastage 56%. M.V.S. arrived at SALEUX.	SM3

WAR DIARY
INTELLIGENCE SUMMARY
(Erase heading not required.)

Army Form C. 2118.

Place	Date	Hour	Summary of Events and Information	Remarks and references to Appendices
SALEUX	7/4/18		Visit ADVS at III Corps Headquarters (Rear). Receive instructions. Reconnoiterinto V.E.S. PICQUIGNY. As the ADVS Corps horses had to be slaughtered during retirement a spy is previous recho AE 9,2000 mes reissued	
"	8.4.18		Unit inspections	
"	9.4.18		Colls J.G.TAYLOR & C.H. SHEATHER return to duly. III Corps ADVS notified	
"	10.4.18		Capt. R.F. STIRLING ALC moved to POIX to join 96: AFA Bgde RMS	
"			notified movement. Unit inspections	
"	11.4.18		Conference NVO's present. Capts SHEATHER, GLYNN, RICHMOND & TAYLOR. arrange Veterinary Changes collection preliminary	
"	12.4.18		Capt PITT H. are reported for duly with 2/290 Bgde. newly returns submitted to III Corps showing horses. Last Ret. 46. Admit 74 Total 120.	
"			Cured 37. Transferred Sick R 21 Died 4. Destroy Rem 57. Total 120. Missing 2. Strength 2593. Wastage 7690. Mules. Last Ret 3. Admit 17. Total 20 Cured 3. Died 4 Destroy 1. Rem 13. Total 20. Strength 1176. Wastage 4170. MVS moved to field	
"			at SALEUX under Canvas. My office moved to tent with M.V.S	
"	13.4.18		Inspected attached labour Groups Coys 4 & 9, Canadian Forestry Corps	

WAR DIARY
or
INTELLIGENCE SUMMARY.
(Erase heading not required.)

Army Form C. 2118.

Instructions regarding War Diaries and Intelligence Summaries are contained in F. S. Regs., Part II. and the Staff Manual respectively. Title pages will be prepared in manuscript.

Stamp: 58th (LONDON) DIVISION (VETERINARY) Date 30/4/18

(91)

Place	Date	Hour	Summary of Events and Information	Remarks and references to Appendices
SALEUX.	13.4.18		Cont'd. Case of Ulcerative Cellulitis admitted into M.V.S. from 32nd Res. Park III Corps. Found on microscopical examination the Spirochete Lymphangitis. Animal destroyed. A.D.V.S. Corps notified by wire. Full particulars sent.	SLB
"	14.4.18		Divisional unit-Inspections. On instructions from A.D.V.S. III Corps Inspected animals of 32nd Res. Park all round treatment cases marked E.C. and placed in working condition. Usual instruction issued.	SLB
"	15.4.18		Case of Spirochete Lymphangitis occurred in mule belonging to detachment of 19 animals belonging to A/291 Trench Mortars attached to No. 2 Sect. D.A.C. Unit inspected, usual instruction carried out. A.D.V.S. notified by wire.	SLB
"	16.4.18		5 privates sent from No. 5 Vety. Hospital reported for temporary duty with M.V.S. These are interveterinary Establishment sent to render assistance during the heavy evacuations. I had pleasure of recommending Staff Sergt. W.M.ALDEN T.O.O.P.I. for the Military Medal on account of his good services during the retirement. Today's Divisional Orders announced that the Corps Commander had much pleasure in presenting the Ribbon.	SLB
"	17.4.18		Usual routine Inspection. Immunization for prevention at M.V.S. visit Inspection.	SLB

WAR DIARY
or
INTELLIGENCE SUMMARY.

(Erase heading not required.)

Army Form C. 2118.

Place	Date	Hour	Summary of Events and Information	Remarks and references to Appendices
SALEUX	15.4.18		S.E. 3109 Pte WARD G. A.V.C. posted temporary with H.Q. D.E. 1 M.G. Battn. for duty with that unit pending the arrival of a Vety Sergeant. Weekly A.F.A 2030 for 5th & 9th Australian Infantry Bgds forwarded to ADVS & 2nd & 3rd Aust. Divs respectively. Conference DDVS.	
"	19.4.18		Weekly returns forwarded to ADVS in Corps. Showing Horses Evac-Rel 67. Admit 92. Total 149. Cured 39. Trans Sic R 35. died 7 Destroy 10. Rem 60 Total 149. Missing 1. Strength 25'02. Mules 1.6.90. Mules kept at 13 Admit 16. Total 29. Cured 11 Trans Sic R 1. died to destroy 4. Rem 10 Total 29. Missing 1. Strength 12'02. Mastage 16670. The DDVS Aus Maj. Gen Moore + ADVS. Ti Corps visits complete the MVS	
"	20.4.18		Instructions received from A.D.V.S. to evacuate BTRs 15 Vety Hosp. Rouen.	
"	21.4.18		Sunfested Div Sig Coy, & R.E. Corps & MVS arrival for evacuation	
"	22.4.18		ASC Corps. + 176. Bgd? Byde +M.V.S. "	
"	23.4.18		D.H.Q + M.M.P & 63rd M.G. Corps & M.V.S. "	
"	24.4.18		D.A.C., 290 Bgde R.F.A, 174 Inf Bgde & M.V.S. "	
"	25.4.18		S/Sergt. ALDEN. W.M. A.V.C. evacuated to Hospital recommend for advancement. Cont.	

Army Form C. 2118.

WAR DIARY
or
INTELLIGENCE SUMMARY.
(Erase heading not required.)

Instructions regarding War Diaries and Intelligence Summaries are contained in F. S. Regs., Part II. and the Staff Manual respectively. Title pages will be prepared in manuscript.

Place	Date	Hour	Summary of Events and Information	Remarks and references to Appendices
SALEUX	25.4.18	Cont.	Senior NCO in a V.E.S. Capt Richmond F.J. Oic. evacuated to 70's CCS suffering from Impetigo Contagiosa of face. Conference D.D.O's	AB
"	26.4.18		Neuber, returns forwarded to A.D.V.S. 1st Corps showing Horse Lost R.1.60 Admit 128 Total 188. Cured 144 Team Sick 23 Died 25 Desty 4. Rem 92 Mules Missing & Recovered 2. Strength 2591. Moortage 2.2 % Mules Lost Rel. 10 Admit 43 Total 53. Cured O Team Sick 3 Died 7 desty 8 Rem 23 Total 53. Strength 1182 Mortage 1.S. % Visited 212st Div Artillery with DDVS 1V army & A.D.V.S 111 Corps. Investigate sickness in the unit. P.M's investigation lead to the opinion it was the result of gas poisoning mostly from drinking water in which gas shells had exploded. Report submitted on the M.R. He trained Skinner attached DM.S showing that during the month he had culled 26 Skins He Recommends that a trained Skinner be permanently attached to Division.	AB
"	27.4.18		Office moves to ST RIQUIER	AB
ST RIQUIER	28.4.18		M.V.S moves from SALEUX to new area billeting for night at HANGEST	SAB
"	29.4.18		M.V.S arrives at new area established at NEUVILLE very good site	SAB

WAR DIARY
or
INTELLIGENCE SUMMARY.

(Erase heading not required.)

Army Form C. 2118.

58th (LONDON) DIVISION
Date 30/4/18
VETERINARY

Place	Date	Hour	Summary of Events and Information	Remarks and references to Appendices
ST RIQUIER	30.4.18		Inspect 58th D Batty. Visit M.V.S. Evacuations by road into ABBEVILLE. During the month Animals Died 57. Destroyed 29. Missing 12. Issued 21. Transferred sick to Base mostly through Mobile Vet Sectns 95. Number Animals evacuated through M.V.S. other than Divisional units 176. Total number evacuated by M.V.S. for month 271.	
			Date of Embarkation 19.1.17.	

J.M.Brunton
Major,
D.A.D.V.S.
58th (LONDON) DIVISION.

Army Form C. 2118.

WAR DIARY
or
INTELLIGENCE SUMMARY (VETERINARY)

(Erase heading not required.)

Instructions regarding War Diaries and Intelligence Summaries are contained in F. S. Regs., Part II. and the Staff Manual respectively. Title pages will be prepared in manuscript.

Place	Date	Hour	Summary of Events and Information	Remarks and references to Appendices
ST RIQUIER	1/5/18		Visit to M.V.S. and inspected animals for evacuation. Inspected Artillery Units.	Sd/s
do	2/5/18		Conference of V.Os. Present Capts SHEATHER GLYNN & TAYLOR. Collection of weekly returns.	Sd/s
do	3/5/18		Case of EPIZOOTIC LYMPHANGITIS occurred in O/201 Bde R.F.A. Animal destroyed after confirmation by microscopical examination, and all the necessary precautions strictly carried out. A.D.V.S. III Corps notified by wire and full particulars on tubes on A.F. W 3738. Weekly returns forwarded to A.D.V.S. III Corps as follows:— "HORSES". On last return 92. Admitted 87. Total 179. Cured 48. Sent to base sick 28. Died 26. Destroyed 9. Remaining under treatment 68. Total 179. Missing 1. Strength 2469. Mortage 2.4%. "MULES". On last return 23. Admitted 31. Total 54. Cured 11. Transferred sick 11. Died 18. Destroyed 2. Remaining under treatment 11. Total 54. Missing 1. Strength 1180. Mortage 2.7%.	Sd/s
do	4/5/18		Inspection of Divisional Units.	Sd/s
do	5/5/18		Capt. D. CAMPBELL A.V.C. (M.C.) reported for duty vice lt Dutton No 5 Vety Hospital.	Sd/s

WAR DIARY or INTELLIGENCE SUMMARY

Army Form C. 2118.

Place	Date	Hour	Summary of Events and Information	Remarks and references to Appendices
ST RIQUIER	5/5/18	Cont'd	Two A.V.C. Sergeants SE.2355. BARRETT.P. attached C/290 Bde R.F.A. and 275. MURTAGH. E.J. attached B/291 Bde R.F.A. evacuated to Hospital and replacements wired for from Base. Case of EPIZOOTIC LYMPHANGITIS in a mule from No 3 Sect 58 D.A.C. Diagnosis confirmed by microscopical examination, animal destroyed and necessary instructions regarding methods of thorough disinfection regionals carried out.	SLs
do	6/5/18		Office moved from ST RIQUIER to MOLLIENS-AU-BOIS. A.D.V.S. notified by wire. M.V.S. also move and stay night at HANGEST. Instructions received from A.D.V.S. III Corps to evacuate animals to Mobile V.E.S. at OLINCOURT CHATEAU.	SLs
MOLLIENS-AU-BOIS	7/5/18		M.V.S. arrive and no locate at PIERREGOT. A.D.V.S. III Corps notified by wire. Instructions issued to Capt C.H. SHEATHER. Jnr C(TC) to proceed forthwith to assume command of No 3. V.E.S. at PONT REMY (vide A.D.V.S III Corps instructions by wire T.395 dated 6/5/18) also to hand over command of 58 Div M.V.S. and inspect a/c to Capt J. CAMPBELL Jnr C (TC).	SLs
do	8/5/18		Capt @ M. SHEATHER proceeds to No.3 V.E.S. PONT REMY. Capt CAMPBELL assumes command of M.V.S. all concerned notified. Capt V.R de BOISCIÈRE. Jnr C (TC) reports for duty, no temporary relief to Capt F.J. RICHMOND M.V.C, and no passes r O/C 58 Div Train. A.D.V.S. III Corps notified by wire.	SLs

WAR DIARY
INTELLIGENCE SUMMARY

Army Form C. 2118.

Place	Date	Hour	Summary of Events and Information	Remarks and references to Appendices
MOLLIENS-AU-BOIS.	9/5/18		Visited and inspected M.V.S. also 511 St Co R.E. Routine Order inserted in D.A.Q. Orders as follows. No. 1051. "ANIMALS FOUND" "Units having recovered horses mules belonging to the French Army or Civilians will forthwith hand the same to the Mobile Veterinary Section". Collection of weekly returns.	AB3
do	10/5/18		Weekly returns forwarded to A.D.V.S. III Corps as follows. HORSES In last return 68. Admitted 115. Total 183. Cured 49 Transferred Sick 55. Died 2 Destroyed 1. Remaining under treatment 76. Total 183. Missing nil. Found 2. Strength. 2461. Wastage 2.2%. MULES In last return 11. Admitted 10 Total 21. Cured 8. Transferred Sick 6 Destroyed 1. Remaining under treatment 6. Total 21. Missing nil. Found 4. Strength. 114. S. Wastage .25%. Inspected 58-Bn M.G. Corps. Tractor M.V.S.	SS4
do	11/5/18		Inspected 143 Inf. Bde. 510 Co A6 2/1 - K6.F.A. also attached units. 305 Rd Construction Co. SS Cable Section R.E.	SS3
do	12/5/18		Inspected 511 Co R.E. and M.V.S.	SS3
do	13/5/18		Inspection of Divisional Units	SS3
do	14/5/18		Visit and inspection of 290, 291 Bdes R.F.A. which have stayed behind in ST RIQUIER Area.	SS3

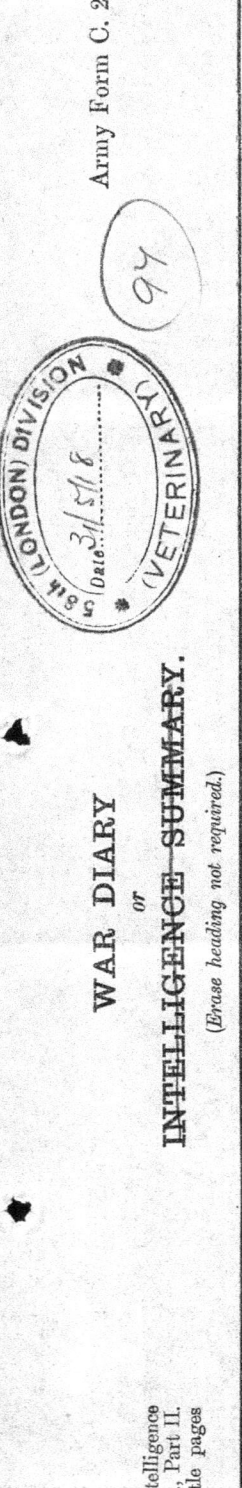

Army Form C. 2118.

WAR DIARY
or
INTELLIGENCE SUMMARY.
(Erase heading not required.)

58th (LONDON) DIVISION
Date 31/5/18.
(VETERINARY)

Place	Date	Hour	Summary of Events and Information	Remarks and references to Appendices
MOLLIENS-AU-BOIS.	15/5/18.		Instructions received from A.D.V.S. III Corps to give Vety attendance to 104 Lab. Co. SE1851 Sergt THRESHER B. AVC reports for duty with C Batty 290 Bde. RFA from No 2 Veterinary Hospital. Inspects M.V.S and Div Units.	S/S
do	16/5/18.		Conference of V.Os. Collection weekly returns. TT.0892 Sergt MCALLAN N. AVC attached to D/290 Bde RFA evacuated to Hospital and replacement wired for from Base.	S/S
do	19/5/18.		Weekly returns submitted to A.D.V.S. III Corps as follows. HORSES On last return 76 Admittes 88 Total 164 Cured 26 Transferred 92 Died & Destroyed 3 Remaining under treatment 39 Total 164 Missing 1 Found 3. Strength 2526 Wastage 3.6%. MULES. On last Return 6. Admittes 21 Total 27 Cured 5 Trans sick 12 Remaining under treatment 10 Total 27 Found 1 Wastage .91%. The Wastage this week is abnormally high on account of evacuations from Artillery Units made to leading of debility. They are animals evacuated by order of A.D.V.S. III Corps. as likely to benefit by a months Convalescent Horse Depot treatment. They are all animals that are making good in its Units but if a heavy call was made upon them they are barely in condition to stand it. Office also A.V.S. move to CONTAY A.D.V.S. III Corps notified by wire.	S/S

Army Form C. 2118.

WAR DIARY
or
INTELLIGENCE SUMMARY.
(Erase heading not required.)

Instructions regarding War Diaries and Intelligence Summaries are contained in F. S. Regs., Part II. and the Staff Manual respectively. Title pages will be prepared in manuscript.

58th (LONDON) DIVISION
Date 31/5/18
(VETERINARY)

Place	Date	Hour	Summary of Events and Information	Remarks and references to Appendices
CONTAY	18/5/18		Instructions received from A.D.V.S. III Corps to give Veterinary attendance to 72nd and 413th Labour Companies.	SS3
do	19/5/18		Inspected 291 Bde R.F.A and 58 D.A.C. 2 Invalids over establishment at M.V.S. despatched to No.19 V.E.S. PICQUIGNY. Inspected 503, 504 & 511 Field Coy RE with the CRE 58 Divn.	S2/13
do	20/5/18		Capt F.J. RICHMOND. M.O(T.F) returns to duty work to Division and is posted V.O.i/c 58 Divn Train. Inspection of Arm Units.	S2/15
do	21/5/18		Capt N.R. de BOSSIÈRE Av.C(T.C) proceeds to 150 R.F.A Bde for duty in accordance with A.D.V.S. III Corps wire T422 dated 12/5/18. Inspected Animals of Divisional Train Units. Sergt HENDERSON. G.J. No TT03298 Av.C. reports for duty with B/291 Bde R.F.A. from No 22 Army Transport Coy. Inspected M.V.S.	S1/15
do	22/5/18		Attends the inspection of Artillery Horses by the Inspector General in Horse-Manship. Inspects Animals at MVS for evacuation.	S2/18
do	23/5/18		Conference of M.O. of D.A.D.V.S. Office. Present Capts CAMPBELL TAYLOR. RICHMOND. GLYNN. Inspected. D/291 Bde R.F.A, also M.V.S.	S2/18
do	24/5/18		Inspects D.A.C. Units, also animals at M.V.S for evacuation.	S2/18

WAR DIARY or INTELLIGENCE SUMMARY

Army Form C. 2118.

Place	Date	Hour	Summary of Events and Information	Remarks and references to Appendices
CONTAY.	24/5/18	Cont	Weekly returns forwarded to A.D.V.S. III Corps as follows. "HORSES" In last return 39. Admitted 94. Total 133. Cured 34. transferred sick 12. Died 8. Destroyed 1. Remaining under treatment 78. Total 133. Missing 3. Found 1. Strength. 2504. Wastage. .91.%. MULES In last return 10. Admitted 14. Total 24. Cured 7. Transferred sick 2. Destroyed 2. Remaining under treatment 13. Total 24. Strength 1135. Wastage. .35%	JS/6 JS/13 JS/15
do.	25/5/18		Inspected 290 Bde R.F.A. and animals at M.V.S. for evacuation.	JS/13
do.	26/5/18		Inspected 14th Inf Bde. 1/4 Suffolk Pioneers, Advanced Wagon Lines of Artillery.	JS/13
do.	27/5/18		Inspected 3 Field Ambulances.	
do.	28/5/18		Inspection of Divisional Units. During the evening 3 horses were killed and 10 slightly wounded by enemy shell fire. The 3 horses killed were the O.C.s 2 chargers & the Staff Sergt Mjrs horse & the very first and have been with M.V.S. since its formation. The shell landed right on the stables, bringing down the whole building & burying the horses. Capt CAMPBELL and his personnel worked splendidly to get them all out and save as much of the stores as possible.	W/6 JS/13
do.	29/5/18		Inspected No.1 Sect. D.A.C. 291 Bde. R.F.A.	

WAR DIARY
or
INTELLIGENCE SUMMARY

Army Form C. 2118.

Place	Date	Hour	Summary of Events and Information	Remarks and references to Appendices
CONTAY	30/5/18		Conference of V.O's present Capts CAMPBELL, RICHMOND, TAYLOR, GLYNN. Inspected 503, 504, 511 Fd Cos R.E. 58 Bn M.G. Corps. 173 Inf Bde.	Sd/s
do	31/5/18		Inspected 509 Co A.S.C. No 2 Sect D.A.C. Weekly returns forwarded to A.D.V.S. III Corps as follows – HORSES In last return 78 Admitted 92 Total 170 Cured 52 Transferred sick 38, Died 6 Remaining under Treatment 74 Total 170 Strength 2504 Wastage 1.7%. MULES In last return 13 Admitted 20 Total 33 Cured 9 Transferred sick 5 Remaining under treatment 19 Total 33 Strength 1130 Wastage .61%.	Sd/s

Date of Embarkation 19-1-17.

[signature]
Major,
D.A.D.V.S.
58th (LONDON) DIVISION.

WAR DIARY
INTELLIGENCE SUMMARY

Army Form C. 2118.

Place	Date	Hour	Summary of Events and Information	Remarks and references to Appendices
CONTAY	1/6/18		Visited and inspected 290 Bde RFA, also animals at M.T. & M. evacuation. Casualty were sent to ADVS III Corps shewing 1 animal killed & 5 wounds from Hostile Bomb.	
do	2/6/18		Office move from CONTAY to MOLLIENS-AU-BOIS. M.S. stay behind at CONTAY. Return forwarded to ADVS III Corps shewing 19 thins valued during the month of May. A big number of these wounds inevitably have been lost not have been no farrier skinner attached to the Division. Casualty were forwarded to ADVS III Corps shewing 8 horses killed 6 wounded by shell fire.	
MOLLIENS-AU-BOIS	3/6/18		Inspected Divisional Units. TT0801 Staff Sergt ALDEN M.M. proceeds to No 3 V.E.S. to duty in accordance with instructions from ADVS III Corps No. 33½g date 1.6.18	
do	4/6/18		Inspected Divisional Units 175 Inf Bde Group.	
do	5/6/18		Instructs to move M.S. and wife is selected at RAINNEVILLE	
do	6/6/18		Conference of M.O.S at my Office — present Capts CAMPBELL, TAYLOR, RICHMOND & GLYNN. Compiling weekly returns Inspected Divl units.	
do	7/6/18		Inspected 143 and 174 Infantry Bde groups complete. Weekly returns	

WAR DIARY
or
INTELLIGENCE SUMMARY.

Army Form C. 2118.

Place	Date	Hour	Summary of Events and Information	Remarks and references to Appendices
MOLLIENS AU BOIS	7/6/18		(Continued) forwarded to A.D.V.S. III Corps as follows "HORSES In Last Return 74. Admitted 92 Total 166. Evac'd 59 Trans sick 42 Died 9 Destroyed 1. Remaining 55 Total 166. Missing 2 Found 4. Strength 2403 Invalids 2%. MULES In Last Return 19 Admitted 12 Total 31. Cured 11 Trans sick 9 Remaining 11 Total 31. Strength 1134 Invalids 78%.	JJB
do	8/6/18		Inspected suspected case of Epizootic Lymphangitis in C Batty 291 Bde R.F.A. Neither the microscopical examination or the clinical symptoms were consistant. Had to M.V.J. at CONTAY.	JJB
do	9/6/18		M.V.J. moved to RAINNEVILLE. Inspected Divisional Units	JJB
do	10/6/18		Office move to CAVILLON. On way to XXII Corps Area. M.V.S. also moved to same Area and is established at BREILLY. A.D.V.S. III Corps ÷ XXII M Corps took notches by mine.	JJB
CAVILLON	11/6/18		Met A.D.V.S. XXII M Corps and received machine known in the rendering of returns and in of charge of Conference at Corps H.Q. Rearrangement of V.O. Charges for present Area	JJB

Army Form C. 2118.

WAR DIARY
or
INTELLIGENCE SUMMARY.
(Erase heading not required.)

Instructions regarding War Diaries and Intelligence Summaries are contained in F.S. Regs., Part II. and the Staff Manual respectively. Title pages will be prepared in manuscript.

Place	Date	Hour	Summary of Events and Information	Remarks and references to Appendices
GAVILLON	12/6/18		Inspected 145 Inf Bde Por Sign & 512 Coy A.S.C.	JKK
do	13/6/18		Conference of N.O.'s present Capts CAMPBELL, GLYNN, TAYLOR & RICHMOND. Inspected 2/1- 2/2- N6 F.A.	JKK
do	14/6/18		Weekly returns submitted to A.D.V.S. XXII nd Corps no. b Horses. Horses. In last Return 55 Admitted 44 Total 129 Cured 42 Transferred sick 18 Died 1. Remaining 68 Total 129. Missing 1. Strength 2523 Wastage 12%. "MULES" In last return 11 Admitted 14 Total 25 Cured 6 Trans sick 6 Remaining 13 Total 25. Found 1. Strength 1149 Wastage 4.3%.	JKK JKK
do	15/6/18		Attended conference at A.D.V.S. XXII nd Corps. Inspected Divl Units.	JKK
do	16/6/18		Visited New Area at BEAUCOURT with reference to taking over from 47th Division.	JKK
do	17/6/18		Visited M.V.S. and arrange move to new area. Inspected Divl Units.	JKK
do	18/6/18		M.V.S. move to BEAUCOURT, A.D.V.S. XXII nd Corps notified	JKK
do	19/6/18		Inspected Divl Units, and Office routine.	JKK
do	20/6/18		Office move to BEAUCOURT. In III Corps Area A.D.V.S. notified. 10.30 conference present Capts GLYNN RICHMOND & Capt P.BELL	JKK

WAR DIARY
or
INTELLIGENCE SUMMARY

Army Form C. 2118.

Place	Date	Hour	Summary of Events and Information	Remarks and references to Appendices
BEAUCOURT	20/6/18 (Cont.)		Instructions received from A.D.V.S. III Corps to give Veterinary attendance to the following Units in Divl. area. 180(T) Coy R.E. 253(T) Coy R.E. 256(T) Coy R.E. Det 4th Cav Army Vet Coy, 409 Inf Co, B+C Cos 108 US Engineers.	JB
do.	21/6/18		Returns submitted to A.D.V.S. III Corps as follows HORSES In End Rev 68 Admitted 42 Total 110 Cured 43 Evan Sick 10 Destroyed 3 Remaining 54 Total 110. Found 1 Strength 2601 Wastage 4.5%. MULES In End return. 13 Admitted 15 Total 28 Cured 10 Evan Sick 2 Remaining 16 Total 28 Wastage 1.8%. 20h 135 Lieut SHARPE L.A.V.C attached to 175 Inf Bn evacuated to Hospital. Replacement wired for from Bde. Casualty wire sent to A.D.V.S. III Corps shewing 6 animals killed, 16 wounded by shell fire.	JB
do.	22/6/18		Inspection of 175 Inf Bde. Visited M.V.S. & inspected animals in evacuation	JB
do.	23/6/18		Inspected A.S.C. Companies.	JB
do.	24/6/18		Inspected Artillery Units R.A.6.	JB
do.	25/6/18		Instructions received from A.D.V.S. III Corps to evacuate all cases of specific Ophthalmia. Inspected Divl Units.	JB

WAR DIARY
or
INTELLIGENCE SUMMARY.
(Erase heading not required.)

Army Form C. 2118.

Place	Date	Hour	Summary of Events and Information	Remarks and references to Appendices
BEAUCOURT.	26/6/18		Inspected 291 Bde R.F.A.	JMB
do	27/6/18		Conference of V.O.s at DADVS Office present Capts RICHMOND GLYNN, CAMPBELL & TAYLOR. Visit to A.D.V.S. III Corps. Inspected Animals at M.V.S. for evacuation.	JMB
do	28/6/18		Weekly returns submitted to ADVS III Corps as follows:- Horses - Week ending Return 54 Admitted 94 Total 148 Cured 42 Evacuated 25 Died 9 Destroyed 1 Remaining 71 Total 148 Missing 2 Found 1 Strength 2635 Wastage 1.3% MULES:- In last Return 16 Admitted 22 Total 38 Cured 12 Evacuated 7 Died 1 Remaining 18 Total 38 Missing nil Found nil Wastage .70% Major General F M RAMSEY, C.M.G. D.S.O. commanding 58 (London) Div. inspects mot. veh. sect. Inspected Animals at M.V.S. for evacuation. Casualty nine.	JMB
do	29/6/18		Sent to ADVS III Corps showing 2 animals wounded by bombs. Inspected Field Ambulances and Animals at M.V.S. for evacuation.	
do	30/6/18		26 Mules have been evacuated by m.v.s during the month, and sent to V.E.S. for handing over to the Bnt. Date of Embarkation 19-1-17.	JMB

RoMBowden Major.
D.A.D.V.S.
58th (LONDON) DIVISION.

WAR DIARY
INTELLIGENCE SUMMARY.

(Erase heading not required.)

Army Form C. 2118.

Place	Date	Hour	Summary of Events and Information	Remarks and references to Appendices
BEAUCOURT	1/7/18		Inspecting Divisional Units. No 641 Sergt COOK J. A.V.C. reports for duty, vice Sergt SHARPE G. A.V.C. evacuated. Inspected animals at M.D.S. for evacuation. Casualties wire despatched to A.D.V.S. III Corps, showing the following Bomb casualties Killed 2 Wounded 6.	JSK
do	2/7/18		Inspecting Divisional Units, also animals at M.D.S. for evacuation	JSK
do	3/7/18		do	JSK
do	4/7/18		Conference of V.O.s at my Office, present Capts RICHMOND, CAMPBELL, GLYNN & TAYLOR. Inspected Divisional Units, and animals at M.D.S. for evacuation.	JSK
do	5/7/18		Weekly returns forwarded to A.D.V.S. III Corps as follows. HORSES. In last return 71. Admitted 58. Total 129. Cured 33. Evac: Sick 41. Died 2. Destroyed 2. Remaining 51. Total 129. Strength 2650. Wastage 1.6%. MULES. In last return 18. Admitted 24. Total 42. Cured 14. Evac: sick 11. Destroyed 1. Remaining 16. Total 42. Strength 1120. Wastage 1.05%.	JSK
do	6/7/18		Inspecting Divisional Units. Animals evacuated thro M.D.S. during the week from 58 Divn 52. Other formations 55. Total 107.	JSK

Army Form C. 2118.

WAR DIARY
or
INTELLIGENCE SUMMARY.
(Erase heading not required.)

Instructions regarding War Diaries and Intelligence Summaries are contained in F.S. Regs., Part II. and the Staff Manual respectively. Title pages will be prepared in manuscript.

58th (LONDON) DIVISION — Date 31/7/18

Place	Date	Hour	Summary of Events and Information	Remarks and references to Appendices
BEAUCOURT	7/7/18		Inspected animals at M.D. for evacuation. Inspected Sgs & 52 Coys A.o.C. VETERINARY	SLB
do	8/7/18		Inspected Divl Units & animals for evacuation.	SLB
do	9/7/18		Inspected 174 & 175 Infantry Bdes. Inspected Animals at M.D.S. for evacuation. Instructions received from A.D.V.S. III Corps to give Veterinary attendance to 74th Labour Coy.	SLB
do	10/7/18		Worked & inspected Artillery Units. Inspected sick animals at M.D.S. for evacuation.	SLB
do	11/7/18		Conference of V.O's, present Capt. RICHMOND, GLYNN, CAMPBELL, TAYLOR. Compiling weekly return. Inspected animals at M.D.S. for evacuation.	SLB
do	12/7/18		Weekly return forwarded to A.D.V.S. III Corps as follows. HORSES. In Lastreturn 51. Admitted 69. Total 118. Cured 28 Trans: Sick to Divn 2. Destroyed 2. Remaining 86. Total 118. Found 1. Strength 2599. WASTAGE 1.9%. MULES. In last return 16. Admitted 19. Total 35. Cured 9. Trans: Sick. 8. Remaining 18. Total 35. Strength 100%. Wastage 1.2%. Animals Evacuated two Sub.V.S. from 58 Divn 58. From other formations 39. Total 97. Inspected animals at M.D.S. for evacuation.	SLB

Army Form C. 2118.

WAR DIARY
or
INTELLIGENCE SUMMARY.
(Erase heading not required.)

Instructions regarding War Diaries and Intelligence Summaries are contained in F. S. Regs., Part II. and the Staff Manual respectively. Title pages will be prepared in manuscript.

Place	Date	Hour	Summary of Events and Information	Remarks and references to Appendices
BEAUCOURT	13/7/18		Inspected 175 Inf Bn Group and Animals at M.V.S. for evacuation. No. 111 S4 Sgt WILBERFORCE G H AVC reported for duty with 58 Bn M.G. Corps.	SLB
do	14/7/18		Inspected Divisional Units. Also animals at M.V.S. for evacuation.	SLB
do	15/7/18		In accordance with D.V.S. instructions asking for a working scheme for Central Clipping of Horses in the Division, my suggestions are submitted to A.D.V.S. III Corps. & a copy given to D.A.Q. Animals inspected at M.V.S. for evacuation.	SLB
do	16/7/18		Inspected Field Coy R.E. also Animals at M.V.S. for evacuation.	SLB
do	17/7/18		Inspected D.A.Q. Group, including M.M.P. Sig Coy, Capt GLYNN M.T. MC 10/10 291 Bn R.F.A. proceeds on 14 days leave to U.K.	SLB
do	18/7/18		Conference of V.Os at my Office. Present Capts RICHMOND, TAYLOR & CAMPBELL. Inspected Divisional Units.	SLB
do	19/7/18		Return submitted to ADVS III Corps as follows. HORSES In last return 36 Admitted 83 Total 119. Cured 22 Evac: sick 51 Destroyed 2 Remaining 44 Total 119. Found 1. Strength 2533 Wastage 306. MULES In last return 18 Admitted 19 Total 35 Cured 10 Evac: sick 7 Dest 2 Remaining 16 Total 35 Strength 1085 Wastage 62%. Animals evacuated during 14 days thro M.V.S. from 58 Bn 58 Other formations 44 Total 102	SLB

(A10266) Wt W5300/P713 750,000 2/18 Sch. 58 Forms/C2118/16 D. D. & L., London, E.C.

Army Form C. 2118.

WAR DIARY
or
INTELLIGENCE SUMMARY.
(Erase heading not required.)

Place	Date	Hour	Summary of Events and Information	Remarks and references to Appendices
BEAUCOURT	19/7/18		Continued DDR & DDVS South Army inspects all 1½ Pack Horses in the Division at Divisional Headquarters, and arranges exchange to mules	JHB
do.	20/7/18		Inspected C/240 Bde R.F.A. C/291 3/291 Bde R.F.A. 1½ Sec. D.A.C. also Animals at M.V.S. for evacuation. Casualty wire forwarded to A.D.V.S. II Corps showing Casualties from Hostile Bombs. Killed 1. Wounded 8. The low percentage of deaths was due to excellent tent protective trenches built in the horse lines.	JHB
do	21/7/18		Inspected 126 Remounts on arrival at PICQUIGNY trained Remounts few. Train also animals at M.V.S. for evacuation	JHB
do	22/7/18		Inspected Machine Gun Battn. and Artillery units	JHB
do	23/7/18		Inspected 175 Inf Bde also Animals at M.V.S. for evacuation	JHB
do	24/7/18		Inspected Divisional Units on instructions of D.D.R. & D.D.V.S. Fourth Army 63 Pack Horses are exchanged for 63 2.D mules at PICQUIGNY.	JHB
do	25/7/18		Conference of V.Os. at my office present Capts RICHMOND TAYLOR & CAMPBELL Works inspected Artillery units.	JHB

Army Form C. 2118.

WAR DIARY
or
INTELLIGENCE SUMMARY.
(Erase heading not required.)

Place	Date	Hour	Summary of Events and Information	Remarks and references to Appendices
BEAUCOURT	26/1/18		Weekly returns forwarded to A.D.V.S. III Corps as follows HORSES Inlast return 44 Admitted 73 Total 117 Cured 39 Evans set. 20. Died 2 Remaining 56 Total 117. Found 1 Strength 2582 Wastage 8.0% MULES. In last return 16 Admitted 19 Total 35 Cured 12 Evans week 7 Destroyed 2 Remaining 14 Total 35. Strength 1174 Wastage 16.% Animals evacuated thro M.V.S. during the week from 5th Div 27 from other formations 26 Total 53.	WB
do	27/1/18		D.D.V.S. Fourth Army visits and inspected "D" Bat "y 291 Bde R.F.A, in which MANGE has been very prevalent. All precautions have been taken to stamp out the disease, and the animals of the Battery are being specially disinfected, with Pig cream Subl.	SDB
do	28/1/18		Inspection of 290 Bde R.F.A. 175 In/ Bde & Div Train.	SDB
do	29/1/18		Inspected Divisional Units & animals at M.V.S. for evacuation	SDB
do	30/1/18		Inspected Divisional Units also animals at M.V.S. for evacuation	SDB
do	31/1/18		do do	SDB
			Number of Sick saluted send to V.E.S. during month 16. Date of Embarkation 19-1-17	

Alfred N Bowden Major,
D.A.D.V.S.
58th (LONDON) DIVISION

Army Form C. 2118.

WAR DIARY
or
~~INTELLIGENCE SUMMARY~~
(Erase heading not required.)

Vol 20

Place	Date	Hour	Summary of Events and Information	Remarks and references to Appendices
BEAUCOURT	1/8/18		Conference of N.O's present Capts CAMPBELL, RICHMOND TAYLOR. Arrangements made with D.A.D.V.S. 12th Divn, about taking over from M.V.S. Inspects animals at M.V.S. for evacuation.	
do	2/8/18		Returns forwarded to A.D.V.S. III Corps as follows "HORSES" In last returns to Admitted 51. Total 107. Cured 41. Evacs: sick 15. Destroyed 2. Remaining 48. Total 107. Missing 2. Found 3. Strength 3583. Wastage .61%. "MULES" In last return 14. Admitted 19. Total 33. Cured 6. Evacs: sick 3. Remaining 20. Total 23. Found 3. Strength 1187. Wastage Nil. Summary of wastage by units no forwarded to D.A.D.V.S. III Corps. Visit to VIGNACOURT arranging site for M.V.S. Inspects sick units.	
do	3/8/18			
QUERRIEU	4/8/18		Office moved to QUERRIEU and M.V.S. moves to VIGNACOURT. A.D.V.S. III Corps notified by wire. Capt GLYNN M.I. reports from 14 days leave in the U.K. The following units are handed over to D.A.D.V.S. 12th Div. who takes over BEAUCOURT AREA. 180 (Fwn) Coy R.E. 256 (Fwn) Coy R.E. 8th Labour Group. 340 Rd Construction Co R.E.	
do	5/8/18		Inspecting sick units.	
do	6/8/18		Visit to VIGNACOURT and inspects sick units.	
do	7/8/18		Inspector of Remounts. Instructions received from A.D.V.S. III Corps to take over the fly change of 88 Labour Coy.	

Army Form C. 2118.

WAR DIARY
or
INTELLIGENCE SUMMARY.
(Erase heading not required.)

58th LONDON DIVISION
31/8/18
(VETERINARY)

Place	Date	Hour	Summary of Events and Information	Remarks and references to Appendices
QUERRIEU	8/8/18		M.V.S. move to QUERRIEU, advance collecting post established at BONNAY, also a mounted patrol to collect any stray or wounded animals. Conference of A.D's present Capts CAMPBELL RICHMOND GLYNN, and TAYLOR. Compiling weekly returns.	S/3 S/3
do	9/8/18		Instructions received from A.D.V.S. III Corps to give vety attendance to 253 (Tun) Coy R.E. and 1st Siege Coy R.A. R.E. Inspected Divl units. Weekly returns forwarded to A.D.V.S. III Corps as follows:- HORSES In last return 48 Admitted. 62. Total 110. Cured 28. Trans: sick 12 Inns & other formations 1. Died 16 Destroyed 3. Remaining 50. Total 110. Missing 20. Forms vet strength 2533. Wastage 1.9%. MULES. In last return. 30 Admitted 27 Total 47 Cured 14 Trans sick 3 Died 9. Remaining 21. Total 47. Missing 6. Strength 1192 Wastage 1.6%. The following of the battle casualties during week. Killed 25. Missing 31. Destroyed 3 Missing 28. Total 77. Wastage by units forwarded to D.M.O S/S	S/3
do	10/8/18		Inspected Divl Units. also animals at M.V.S. for evacuation. A.D.V.S. III Corps instructs that vety attendance be given to 713 L.A. Coy.	L/S
do	11/8/18		Inspected Divl Unit, also animals at M.V.S. for evacuation.	S/3
do	12/8/18		Inspection of Divl Units. No T.T. 0894 P/a/Cpl CURBISHLEY. P. 58 Div M.V.S. changed with Dunkirne to Reverts to Rank". No SE 23850 U/A/LCpl ABRAHAM.S. recommended & Dunkirne Full. til vacancy. Approval for this obtained from A.D.V.S. III Corps. S/3	S/3

Army Form C. 2118.

WAR DIARY
or
INTELLIGENCE SUMMARY
(Erase heading not required.)

(113)

Stamp: 58TH (LONDON) DIVISION (VETERINARY) 31/8/18

Place	Date	Hour	Summary of Events and Information	Remarks and references to Appendices
ST GRATIEN	13/8/18		Office move to ST GRATIEN. Inspected Sick Units. Capt TAYLOR J.G. V.O.I/C. 290 Bde R.F.A. evacuated to hospital with appendicitis. Reinforcement received for.	L&B
do	14/8/18		Inspected Sick Units. D.T.S. and D.D.V.S. 4th Army inspected M.V.S. at QUERRIEU.	L&B
do	15/8/18		Conference of V.O's, compiling weekly returns. Inspected Sick Units.	L&B
do	16/8/18		Weekly returns submitted to A.D.V.S. III Corps as follows. HORSES In last return 50. Admitted 96. Total 146. Cured 38. Trans. sick 42. Died 24. Remaining 42. Total 146. Missing 3. Found 6. Wastage 2.5%. MULES In last Return 21. Admitted 39. Total 60. Cured 16. Trans. sick 9. Died 13. Destroyed 5. Remaining 19. Total 60. Missing – Found 1. Wastage 1.9%. Battle Casualties during week. Evacuated 73. Killed 39. Destroyed 12. 5. Evacuated 22. Remaining 9. Total 73. Gassed Cases 12.	L&B L&B
do	17/8/18		Inspected Sick Units, and animals of M.T. for evacuation.	L&B
do	18/8/18		Inspection of Sick Units. Lieut. P McLAUGHLIN AVC reported for duty from 5 V.H. and so proto V.O.I/C. 290 Bde R.F.A. vice Capt. J.G. TAYLOR.	L&B
do	19/8/18		Inspection of Divisional Units, also animals at M.V.S. for evacuation.	L&B
do	20/8/18		do	L&B

Army Form C. 2118.

WAR DIARY
or
INTELLIGENCE SUMMARY.

(Erase heading not required.)

Instructions regarding War Diaries and Intelligence Summaries are contained in F. S. Regs., Part II. and the Staff Manual respectively. Title pages will be prepared in manuscript.

58th (LONDON) DIVISION
Date 31/8/18
(VETERINARY)

Place	Date	Hour	Summary of Events and Information	Remarks and references to Appendices
ST GRATIEN	21/8/18		Inspection of Div: Units, also animals at M.V.S. for evacuation	LL/S
do	22/8/18		Conference of O's present Capts CAMPBELL. D. GLYNN. RICHMOND. LIEUT. McLAUGHLIN. Compiling weekly returns.	LL/6
do	23/8/18		Weekly returns forwarded to A.D.V.S. III Corps as follows. HORSES. In last return 42. Admitted 66. Total 108. Cured 38. Evac. sick 13. Died 3. Destroy. 1. Remaining 53. Total 108. Found 2. Strength. 24+8. Wastage .60%. MULES. In last return 19. Admitted 19. Total 38. Cured 13. Evac. sick + Died 1. Destroyed 1. Remaining 19. Total 38. Found 1. Wastage 4.1%. Battle casualties for week 9. Killed Gunshot 3. Evacuated + Remaining 2. Total 9. Summary of Wastage by units forwarded to D.D.O. Instructions received from A.D.V.S. III Corps to give 24/7 attendance to 2nd Life Gds M.G. Regt, which is in working isolation due to EPIZOOTIC LYMPHANGITIS.	QR/5
HEILLY	24/8/18		Office move to HEILLY. Inspecting Div: Units	QR/K
do	25/8/18		M.V.S. move to HEILLY. Inspecting Div: Units.	QR/5
do	26/8/18		Inspection of Div: Units, also animals at M.V.S on evacuation. A.D.V.S III Corps notified that all cases STOMATITIS CONTAGIOSA to reported by wire.	QR/6
do	27/8/18		M.V.S. moved to MORLANCOURT. A.D.V.S. III Corps and D.D.O. notified.	QR/5

Army Form C. 2118.

WAR DIARY
or
INTELLIGENCE SUMMARY.
(Erase heading not required.)

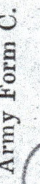

Instructions regarding War Diaries and Intelligence Summaries are contained in F.S. Regs., Part II. and the Staff Manual respectively. Title pages will be prepared in manuscript.

Place	Date	Hour	Summary of Events and Information	Remarks and references to Appendices
MORLANCOURT A.M.A.	28/8/18		Office move to K.14.T sheet 62.D. (South of MORLANCOURT.) Inspecting Div. Units.	QR/8
do	29/8/18		Conference of V.O.'s. Present: Capts CAMPBELL RICHMOND GLYNN also Lieut McLAUGHLIN. Inspecting Div. Units.	QR/3
do	30/8/18		Office move to new Location L.1.7 sheet 62.D. (North West BRAY-sur-Somme.) Weekly returns submitted to A.D.V.S. III Corps as follows HORSES. Sick Return 53. Admitted 81. Total 134. Trans sick 23. Died 15. Destroy 6. Remaining 54. Total 134. Shrink 24.9b. Moving 1.7%. MULES. In last return 19. Admitted 24. Total 43. Cure 11. Trans sick 9. Died 3. Destroyed 2. Remaining 18. Total 43. Shrink 11%. Moving 1.0%. Battle casualties this week. Gunshot 42. Killed 15. Destroys v. Evacuees. 9. Remaining 11. Total 42. Bomb 5. Killed 2. Evacuees 1. Remaining 2. Total 5. List of Moving by Units forwarded to D.H.Q.	QR/8
do	31/8/18		H.Q. moves forward to BRONFAY FARM (F29.7.6.2 sheet 62.D) Date of embarkation 19-1-17.	QR/8

Mair
D.A.D.V.S.
58th (LONDON) DIVISION.

WAR DIARY or **INTELLIGENCE SUMMARY**
(Erase heading not required.)

Army Form C. 2118.

D.A.D.V.S.
58TH DIVISION.
No. ....
Date 30.9.18.

Instructions regarding War Diaries and Intelligence Summaries are contained in F.S. Regs., Part II. and the Staff Manual respectively. Title pages will be prepared in manuscript.

Place	Date	Hour	Summary of Events and Information	Remarks and references to Appendices
MORLANCOURT AREA	1.9.18	—	Inspection of Divisional Units. Bombing mostly at night. Balle Richmond, P.J. A.V.C. (T.R.) proceeds on 14 days leave to United Kingdom	
—do—	2.9.18	—	Enquired into subject EPIZOOTIC LYMPHANGITIS in Div. Units area 8 April 1918. Post-mortem on mule. No mention of ADVS III Corps units (possibly was evacuated)	
—do—	3.9.18	—	Inspection of Div. Units. Casualty Horse evacuated to ADVS III Corps. Matey? Bombs fell 12 evacuated 3	
—do—	4.9.18	—	Inspected Central Dumps	
—do—	5.9.18	—	Captures by K.O.S.B. Captains CAMPBELL and BROWN Lt MCLAUGHLIN Divisional	
—do—	6.9.18	—	Three Returns submitted to ADVS III Corps as follows:— HORSES on hand return Cavalry 42, Lt.draught riding 154, Total 154, Heavy draught 45, Total 45, Draught 17, Dismount 45, Pack draught 2380, Remounts since last return 1 Total 74, Pack 43, Total 154, MULES Pack draught 1, Riding 2, Total 2, Dismount 1, Remount 1, Total 18 Remount April 26. Draught 5, Riding 728/1 Remount 6, 18, Total 44, Remount 15, Evacuated sick 9 Died 2, Destroyed 1, Remounts 17. Total 44, Strength 117 18, Percents 1/18, Strength Battle Casualties Died Sept 22. Killed 18, Wounded 7, Remounts 7, Remount 122. Strength 28 Killed 13 Destroyed 2, Evacuated 2 Remounts 1, Total 23.	
MAUREPAS	7.9.18	—	Office moves to MAUREPAS B.15.A.95. Shell 629 M.V.S. moves to C.20.C. Central Sub S (SUCC.HAYESNESS) Inspection of Div.Units — Ammunition recount M.V.S. to consolidated, Shells 6 ammunition returned from A.D.V.S. Books to Sr.D. d/R 8 Div.Artillery attd. to 58th Div.	
—do—	8.9.18	—	Inspection of Div. Units — amounts at M.V.S.	
—do—	9.9.18	—	Casualty Horse Returned E.G.DVAC III order shewing Casualty animals from July to August 1918 34 wounded 24. Total 58	
—do—	10.9.18	—	Office moves to NURLU AREA d.2.a.2. Clearance all evacuated except Batteries (X(34))	
—do—	11.9.18	—	Weekly return submitted to ADVS III Corps as follows:— Brought. P.Sd up forward for Remounts 3 Remounts 35 4/1 Total 178 Cav 123 Total 54, Diet 24. Brazing 24443. Ramount 23A Died/Dist Cast 174 Total 14 17 animal 11 Total 37, Total 54, Strength 1195. Percents 1/17, Ration 8 Saddles ... Remounts 71.7	
NURLU AREA	12.9.18	—	Killed 42, Destroyed 7 Evacuated 1, Remounts 147, 8 Total 17. Remounts 71.7	
—do—	13.9.18	—	Destroyed 2, Evacuated 7. 8 Total 17. Remounts 11 Rount 6	

WAR DIARY or INTELLIGENCE SUMMARY

Army Form C. 2118.

D.A.D.V.S. 58TH DIVISION

Place	Date	Hour	Summary of Events and Information	Remarks and references to Appendices
NURLU AREA	13-9-18	8 a.m.	Suspected case of EPIZOOTIC LYMPHANGITIS in C. Battery 290th R.F.A. Smear [illegible] negative	
–do–	14-9-18		D.D.V.S. 4th Army and A.D.V.S. III Corps inspected C/290th Bde R.F.A.	
–do–	15-9-18		Inspection of Divnl. details & animals at M.V.S. for evacuation. Return of strays	
–do–	16-9-18		Proposed exchange horses 6th D.A.C.	
–do–			Proposal of Suspect E.L. Mule Destroyed. Animal from unit of 7th ATK Bn Bde Destroyed from Batt 135. Killed 3. Wounded 10. T.P.L. 13	
–do–	17-9-18		Inspection of Divn. Units also 100th Bde Meat Supply Depot inspected	
–do–	18-9-18		Inspection of Bde. Units. Phos Annual at 11 V.S. for evacuation	
–do–	19-9-18		Lecture of B.V.Os. present. CAMPBELL, GLYNN and MEEKE, Lt McLACHLAN	
–do–	21-9-18		Weekly return submitted to A.D.V.S. III Corps re [illegible] return. HORSES 82 / MULES 60	
			Animals Sick 174. Total 256. Strength 2376. Transferred sick 145. Died 4. Destroyed 7. Remount 38. Total 256. Missing 5. Found 5. Strength 2376	
			6.3.1. MULES. In last return 18. Admitted sick 33. Total 51. Transferred sick 15. Died 4. Remounted 19. Total 51. Strength 1302	
			Horses 1.3.1. Battle casualty. Lambs 20. Killed 8. Destroyed 2. Bolt 2. Remounted 1.3. Total 20. Bolt 13. Killed 3. Damaged 1. Trans 7. Total 13. Lame. Horses A.P.C. reported No 2. Veterinary evac. [illegible] Field Units	
			M.V.S. moves to D.14.d.91. Sick 620. Stray horses N. T.7. a.91. M.V.S. [illegible] 4th Army + [illegible] to D. 11. a. 9	
–do–	21-9-18		Inspection of Divn Units and M.V.S. N. T.7. a.915. M.V.S. [illegible] to No 2. Veterinary hospital for evacuating via Syd M.V.C.	
–do–	22-9-18		Purchase ESCRAHAM, £3 are despatched to	
–do–	23-9-18		Inspection of Divn Units	
–do–	24-9-18		Office moves to Battalion Valley, MONTAUBAN	
MONTAUBAN	25-9-18		M.V.S. moves to MONTAUBAN A.D.V.S. III Corps animals Divn. Artillery animals	
M+NAGOYAL	26-9-18		Office moves to MINGOYAL moving VIII Corps area. We saw Artillery [illegible]	
			behind III Corps area	
–do–	27-9-18		M.V.S. moving in VIII Corps area and is established in MUGOYAL. Capt R.E. MENDZT arrives back from leave	

WAR DIARY
or
INTELLIGENCE SUMMARY.
(Erase heading not required.)

Army Form C. 2118.

D.A.D.V.S.
50TH DIVISION
No. ....
Date 30.9.18

Place	Date	Hour	Summary of Events and Information	Remarks and references to Appendices
MINGOVAL	27.9.18	6 a.m.	Returns submitted to A.D.V.S. VIII Corps as follows. 38 Animals sick since 58. Total 96. Evac'd 37. Transferred sick 19. Died 5. Destroyed 7. Remains 24. Total 92. Horses 73. Transit 24/14. March 1.31 MILES. Sick horses return 19. Admitted will 25 Field 49. Brit'd 19. Transport sick 6. Dest 5. Remaining 14. Transport sick 12.9. Wastage 28.). Bn RA casualties. Remain 30. Cond'd 10. Destroy 7. Evac'd 4. Remain 9. Total 30.	
-do-	28.9.18	—	Conference of Div. Vets. Os. held 9. to A.D.V.S. VIII Corps.	
-do-	29.9.18	—	Visit to D.A.D.V.S. 2nd Div. reference taking over new area.	
-do-	30.9.18	—	D.A.D.V.S. proceeded in charge to area 9 handed to Marshal Kingston officers & B.R.S. mobile V.S. Goodwyn — Sgt Y.C.F.I.S.S. Sect'n 2 RICHMOND taken out to joining parade as D.A.D.V.S.	

Weekly Return — Ration 19.1.17

J. Ashenhurst Capt.
For. Major,
L.A.D.V.S.
58th (LONDON) DIVISION.

WAR DIARY or INTELLIGENCE SUMMARY

Army Form C. 2118
D.A.D.V.S. 58th Division

Place	Date	Hour	Summary of Events and Information	Remarks and references to Appendices
SAINS EN GOHELLE	1/10/18		Inspection of Dent Units visited M.V.S.	
do	2/10/18		Inspection of Dent Units. Office Routine	
do	3/10/18		Lt. McKelvey's company. Mackey returned. Y.O's Inspections held out Capts. GLYNN, CAMPBELL, Lieut. McLAUGHLIN. Inspected A.S.C. t/o, 573 M.G. Bn.	
do	4/10/18		Inspected div. sup col. 2/2 Bgde. M.V.S. Mackey returned, completed to A.D.V.S. VIII Corps inspection. HORSES In Instruction 137. Casualties sick 13. Total 47. Evac. 5. Transferred to veterinary 25. Remaining 17 sick, 17 mange. Shrapnel 1196. MULES In Last Return 173. Attached since 8. Total 22. Evac 8. remained 0 others purposes. 6. Died 1. Remaining 7. Total 22. Strength 654. Wastage 1.65%	
do	5/10/18		Inspected 174 Inf Bde + M.G. Bn. A.D.V.S. VIII Corps arrived, 175 Inf Bde + 2/2 H.C.F.A.	
do	6/10/18		Inspected A.S.C. + t/o	
do	7/10/18		Visited M.V.S.	
do	8/10/18		Inspected 173 + 174 Inf Bdes. t/o's + 9401 Coys.	
do	9/10/18		Inspected 573 M.G. Bn.	
do	10/10/18		Visited t/o Shrapshury. McCall returned. V.O's Conference present Capts. GLYNN, CAMPBELL, LIEUT. McLAUGHLIN.	
do	11/10/18		Mackey returned on attached to A.D.V.S. XIII Corps a.o. to fill up. HORSES In war total. 17. Posted 27, t.o. 39, Evac 3. Transferred sick 8. Remaining 71. Total 38. Strength 1143. Wastage 6.96. MULES In Last Return 7. Admitted 14. t.o. 21. Evac. 3. Bumalt 3. Transferred sick 8. Died 2. Remaining 9. Total 21. Strength 643. Wastage 1.3%. Kept 2nd Divl Artillery	

WAR DIARY
or
INTELLIGENCE SUMMARY.

(Erase heading not required.)

Army Form C. 2118.

D.A.D.V.S.
58TH DIVISION

Place	Date	Hour	Summary of Events and Information	Remarks and references to Appendices
TALUS EN GOHELLE	12/9/18		Posted M.V.S. Offer Bonhire	
	13/9/18		Office moved to LES BREBIS	
LES BREBIS	14/9/18		Attended three driving Parade at BOYEFFLES. Inspected 173/174 Coy. R.E. Visit of A.D.V.S. 1st CORPS.	
	5/9/18		M.V.S. move to LES BREBIS. Major T. Scott Howden D.A.D.V.S. reports by wire arrival at BOULOGNE. No T.03798 Scott Henderson G.S. attached to 13/247 Bgde R.F.A. received a Peshawar reinforcement reported from Base	
—do—	16/9/18		Office moved to MONTIGNY. Visited H.Q. tents.	
—do—	17/9/18		Relieved by Lieut. Anstey. Inspected spare VO's of Luere's Brand Boy's FLYNN, CAMPBELL, LIEUT. MCGOVERN	
—do—	18/9/18		Office moved to MONCHEAUX. Having been attached to 6. A.D.V.S. 1st CORPS enjoyed HORSES, on Instructions 73. Remained until 5th. TOTAL 131. Transferred such 36. Died 4. Destroyed 1. Remaining 57. Total 5. 131. 32. Transferred since 21. on Instructions 43 admitted since 21.	
			Imp. 17. 22. 94. Horses 1.17. MULES. Imp. 24. Total 44. admitted 1.24.10. Total 44. Evacuated 16. Transferred in Remaining 24. Total 44. admitted 1.24.10. Wastage 30%.	
			Office move to HERSEE. Your attention invited to A.D.M.S. 1st CORPS C.V./21/206 paras 6. all necessary information of 242 Army Bde R.F.A. + renders necessary steps to indicate her own. Have much more since accordingly to VOI.	
MONCHEAUX	19/9/18			
HERSEE	20/9/18		RADLE M.V.S. M.V.S. moved to PUYCHEUX notice T. Scott Henden D.V.S. arrived at JAIG. notifies A.D.V.S. 1st CORPS by wire. Taken over duties from East Richmond. Lieut. C.G. HEARN A.V.C. R.G.C. 242 Army Bde R.F.A. informed of this office and now reports are such I influence of his services	

WAR DIARY or INTELLIGENCE SUMMARY

Army Form C. 2118.

D.A.D.V.S. 58th DIVISION.

Place	Date	Hour	Summary of Events and Information	Remarks and references to Appendices
KORSEE	25/11/18		M.V.S. moved to BERSÉE. Inspection of M.V.S.	
- do -	28/10/18		Office moved to PLANARD. Heard from Lt Col. HEARNE DDVS of A.D.V.S H Corps with information that No.13 V.E.S. unable to be moved forward to new rendezvous owing to sickness or epizootic amongst mules.	SS6
PLANARD	29/10/18		Inspected DMS tent Antwerpen accepted from Russ that No.56 M.V.S. Capt CHAMBERS 3 A.V.C. R[H]? Who were evacuated from No.2 Veterinary Hospital to 73/81 Bde R.F.A. Visit Bvt HENDERSON evacuated 15/9/81 — to C.R.S. continuing sick. Hospital returns 408 conference present is at 16.	SS6
			Riding Klo. 92nd CAMPBELL HEARN in McLAUGHLIN.	SS8
- do -	24/10/18			
- do -	27/10/18		Reviews submitted C.A.D.V.S. 11th Corps 3rd point HORSES for same time 58. permitted and 52. Total 110 but of these 21 Died 7 Destroyed 1. Remaining 52. Total 110. Strength 24, 8. Mortality 12% Mules Inspection/24 Admitted 18. Total 42. Bugler 16. Transport out 1. Purchase 21. Total 42 Cont 1777. Morgan 30g. East 141.7. 290 364. R.F.A. 9. Cont. M.9. S.L.V.M. Div L.M. 291 422. R.F.A Reviews and rulings expand Nov.5 IRELAND granted under A.C.I.2337 from 27/10/18 Bulletin 58 A.84 of this Corps. Corresp to meet at dressings two mile to one F.Y.03. A.D.V.S. 2/1. H.C.F.A 318 C. + H.G. group. Inspected fixing sheds. 1st CORPS notified to	SS8
			Office sub-here field delivered from M.V.S.	SS8
- do -	26/10/18			SS6
- do -	27/10/18		M.V.S. moved to NOMAIN. Inspected M.V.S. 91 Bde. R.F.A 02+12 Bdes (Lh Bgds)	SS6
- do -	28/10/18		Visit 173 Inf Bde	SS6
- do -	29/10/18		Visit 5th M.G. But R.E. Engr.	SS6
- do -	30/10/18			SS6
- do -	31/10/18		Following + continuing usually promoted KOs conference meets Capts RICHMOND CAMPBELL HEARN + Lt McLAUGHLIN.	SS6

Dates of Inspection 19-1-17

[signature] Major A.D.V.S.
58th (LONDON) DIVISION

Army Form C. 2118.

WAR DIARY
or
INTELLIGENCE SUMMARY.
(Erase heading not required.)

D.A.D.V.S.
58' (LONDON) DIVISION

Place	Date	Hour	Summary of Events and Information	Remarks and references to Appendices
MOUCHIN-PLANARD	1-11-18		Office Routine. Inspection H.Q. Grooms	
- do -	2-11-18		Inspection 290' Bde R.F.A and 58' D.A.C.	
- do -	3-11-18		Inspection 58' M.G Battalion and 291' Bde R.F.A	
- do -	4-11-18		Inspection Sup. TRAIN visit 58' M.V.S	
- do -	6-11-18		Inspection Infantry Brigades	
- do -	7-11-18		Conference of Veterinary Officers and concluding weekly Returns. Present Capts RICHMOND and CAMPBELL, Lt. McLAUGHLIN and CAPT. HEARN. V.O. 4/c 242 A.F.A. BDE.	
BLEHARIES	8-11-18		Office moved to BLEHARIES with D.H.Q. weekly Returns submitted to A.D.V.S. 1st CORPS showing :- HORSES last Return 51. admitted 64. TOTAL 115. Cured 25. Evacuated Sick 18. Died 17. Remaining 55. TOTAL 115. Strength 2234. Wastage 1.57%. MULES last Return 18. admitted 11. TOTAL 29 cured 7. evacuated sick 3. evacuated 1. Remaining 18. TOTAL 29 Strength 1297. Wastage 30%	
- do -	9-11-18		Arrive M.V.S. which moved to RUMEGIES	
- do -	11-11-18		Visit BELOEIL and select new site for M.V.S	
BELOEIL	12-11-18		Office moves to BELOEIL with D.H.Q. M.V.S. moves to BELOEIL	
- do -	13-11-18		Office Routine and inspection of M.V.S	
- do -	14-11-18		Conference of V.O's and concluding weekly Returns. Present CAPTS RICHMOND & CAMPBELL and LT. McLAUGHLIN	
- do -	15-11-18		Returns submitted to A.D.V.S. 1st CORPS showing :- HORSES last Return 55. admitted 22. TOTAL 77. Cured 20. evacuated Sick 3. Died 2. Strayed 1. Remaining 41. TOTAL 77. Strength 1376. Wastage 7.27%. MULES last Return 18. admitted 17. TOTAL 35. Cured 7. evacuated Sick 8. Died 2. Remaining 20. TOTAL 35. Strength 1206. Wastage 6.57%	

WAR DIARY
or
INTELLIGENCE SUMMARY.

(Erase heading not required.)

Army Form C. 2118.

D.A.D.V.S.
58' (LDN) DIVISION

Place	Date	Hour	Summary of Events and Information	Remarks and references to Appendices
BELOEIL	15-11-18		Continued. Report submitted to A.D.V.S. 1st Corps. Reporting that foot and mouth disease exists in most of the villages of the Survervoial Area. Infection spread by a herd of 200 Cattle brought into the area by the Germans all of which were slaughtered at GROSAGE. The outbreak is apparently dying out. 3rd South Em R.E. and 3rd Lon Regt. 3 Horses shot Several cases of contact poisoning in 3rd South Em R.E. and 3rd Lon Regt. 3 Horses shot in Latter Unit. Post Mortem examined the diagnosis of ain inhalant poisoning. Inspection of the forage revealed large quantities of Castor and Broom air Beans in the oats. A.D.V.S. 1st Corps notified by wire and obtained Report forwarded	JSM/S
- do -	16-11-18		Notification received that CAPT M. GLYNN pounced General Service Leave to 14 days from 27-10-18 had been transferred to Home Command. A.D.V.S. 1st Corps notified and reinforcement required. War Diary for Action forwarded to B.H.Q. Further deaths from Bean poisoning and injured A.D.V.S. 1st Corps by wire to inspect the Unit. Diary from A.D.V.S. 1st Corps who was quite satisfied that deaths were the result of Croton and Broom Bean poisoning. O.C. Divisional Train was notified to carefully continue the forage for the presence of Beans the A.D.V.S. taken a sack of oats containing the beans to forward it to the Base for then inspection and received further issue of one poisonous food.	JSM/S
- do -	17-11-18		Visited QUESNOY and inspected Cattle for foot and Mouth disease report of inspection forwarded to A.D.V.S. 1st Corps.	JSM/S
- do -	18-11-18		Court of Enquiry held upon sudden death of many animals in the 1st Lon Regt. from Castor and Broom air Bean poisoning. CAPT CAMPBELL detached to attend as member of the Court. LT McLAUGHLIN received orders regarding sudden serious illness of his father and submits application for special leave to Ireland. The same forwarded to A.D.V.S. 1st Corps.	JSM/S
- do -	19-11-18		Shoeing Smith requested from BASE for M.V.S. 1st replace NO.T.T.0891 S/S STEWART.J. A.V.C. evacuated to hospital.	JSM/S

Continued

Army Form C. 2118.

D.A.D.V.S
58' (LONDON) DIVISION

WAR DIARY
or
INTELLIGENCE SUMMARY.
(Erase heading not required.)

Instructions regarding War Diaries and Intelligence Summaries are contained in F. S. Regs., Part II. and the Staff Manual respectively. Title pages will be prepared in manuscript.

Place	Date	Hour	Summary of Events and Information	Remarks and references to Appendices
BELOEIL	19-11-18		Continued further report to A.D.V.S. 1st Corps on Cresol and Cresol Poisoning showing deaths to date to be as follows:- 3. R. 5 L.D. 7 H.Q. and 1. Mule in the 7' Lon Regt. I.L.D. in 511 Coy R.E. I.L.D. 4' Support Regt I.L.D. 50a Coy R.E. TOTAL 19. All Post Mortems found conclusively to be on poisoning. A further D.R.O. produced suggesting sieving the Oats on spreading out on a tarpaulin to detect the presence of Beans	JRS
-do-	20-11-18		LT E.S. NOTTING, A.V.C. Reported for duty and posted as V.O to 291st Bde, R.F.A. A.D.V.S noted by wire.	JRS JRS
PERUWELZ	21-11-18		Office moved to PERUWELZ with D.H.Q.	
-do-	22-11-18		Conference at this Office present CAPTS. RICHMOND and CAMPBELL LTS McLAUGHLIN and NOTTING accepting and completing weekly Returns and re-arrangement of duties	JRS
-do-	23-11-18		Weekly Returns forwarded to A.D.V.S. 1st Corps showing Horses and Returns 41 admitted 66 TOTAL 107. Cured 24. Cast 19. Destroyed 3 Remaining 51. TOTAL 107. Strength 2378. Wastage 1.2%. Mules last Return 20. Admitted 7. TOTAL 27. Cured 12. Evacuated Sick 1. Died 1. Remaining 13. TOTAL 27. Strength 1147. Wastage .14%. LT McLAUGHLIN granted 14 days' Special Leave from 26" inst.	JRS
-do-	26-11-18		Instructions received from A.D.V.S. 1st Corps that in future all cases of Specific Ophthalmia will be shown under Class II and now class II a Cataracts. Commenced inspection of all animals in a March to bring before a committee at a later date to select Brood Mares	JRS
-do-	28.11.18		Conference of Veterinary Officers present CAPTS. Richmond and Campbell and LT NOTTING. Completing weekly Returns	JRS

Army Form C. 2118.

D.A.D.V.S
58 (LON) DIVISION

WAR DIARY
or
INTELLIGENCE SUMMARY.
(Erase heading not required.)

Place	Date	Hour	Summary of Events and Information	Remarks and references to Appendices
PERUWELZ	29.11.18		Weekly Returns submitted to A.D.V.S. 101Cwts showing: Horses hard Return 5) Admitted 157 Total 108, Cured 46, Evacuated Sick 12, Died 2, Destroyed 1. Remaining 57 Total 108. Strength 2379, Wastage 670, Mules Hd. Return 12, Admitted 11 Total 23 Cured 12, Evacuated Sick 2 Remaining 9 Total 23 Strength 1210, Wastage 1690. M.V.S. moved to No 134 RUE DE SONDEVILLE PERUWELZ and all concerned notified. Date of Embarkation 19.1.1.17	

Signature

Major,
D.A.D.V.S.
58th (LONDON) DIVISION.

Army Form C. 2118.

WAR DIARY
or
INTELLIGENCE SUMMARY.
(Erase heading not required.)

D.A.D.V.S.
58th DIVISION

Place	Date	Hour	Summary of Events and Information	Remarks and references to Appendices
PERUWELZ.	1/12/1918.		Inspection of Divisional Units. Office Routine.	
- do -	2/12/1918.		Inspecting Divisional Units. Weekly M.V.S. General Routine.	
- do -	3/12/1918.		do	
- do -	4/12/1918.		Conference of A.D's. Deputy Chairman CAMPBELL, RICHMOND, Lieut. NOTTING. Weekly returns compiled. Inspected 4th Suffolk Batt'n.	
- do -	5/12/18.		Weekly returns submitted to A.D.V.S. 1st Corps as follows:- horses. In last return 57. Admitted 38 Total 89. Cured 20. Transferred 2. Died. 1. Destroys 2. Remaining Dr. Total 89. Strength 2262. Wastage 67%. Mules. In last return of 13 total 22 Cured 1 Transferred 3 Remaining 18 total 22 Strength 1216. Wastage 24%. Inspects Divisional Units in Brass Mares.	
- do -	6/12/18.		General routine, inspecting Divisional Units.	
- do -	7/12/18		do	
- do -	8/12/18		General routine, the BRIXTON A.B. S/32209. A.D.C. reports to resume duty as clerk to this office.	
- do -	9/12/18.		Inspection of Divisional Units.	
- do -	10/12/18		Visits 1st Remount Section at DOUAI to collect 2 chargers for G.O.C. 58th Division.	

D. Campbell
Capt.

WAR DIARY or INTELLIGENCE SUMMARY

Army Form C. 2118.

D.A.D.V.S.

Place	Date	Hour	Summary of Events and Information	Remarks and references to Appendices
PERNELZ	11/12/1918		Inspection of Divisional Units and General Routine. Conference of A.D.V.S. Present Capt. CAMPBELL RICHMOND. Lieut MOTTING.	
do.	12/12/18		do	
			Weekly returns submitted to A.D.V.S. 1 Corps, as follows:- HORSES. In last return 54 Admitted 49 Total 191 Evac 24 Evac to Convalescent Depôt. Destroyed 5 Remaining 50 Total 191. Strength 2350. Evac. 1. M/Strength 1.9%. MULES. In last return 18 Admitted 11 Total 29. Evac. 2. Evac to Convalescent 5. Remaining 20 Total 29. Strength 1215. Evac. age. 40%.	
do	13/12/18		My inspection of the Divl Units & attached Army field artillery Btie for Road Survey is complete, am on visit of 191 Animals as submitted to A.D.V.S. for parading on R to Evac.	
do	14/12/18		Attended the inspection of Bros there at BAVECLES Special Committee comprises as follows. Lt-Col. T.R.A. McDOUGALL. A.D.V.S. 1 Corps. Major H.O'S. T. TANNER. Storemaster. 1 Corps. Capt. K. WALKER. V.O.1. Remount Depôt. In all 23 animals were selected.	
do	15/12/18		Inspection of Divl Units & Office routine	
do	16/12/18		do	

J. Campbell Capt.

WAR DIARY
or
INTELLIGENCE SUMMARY.
(Erase heading not required.)

Army Form C. 2118.

D.A.D.V.S. 58th Division

Place	Date	Hour	Summary of Events and Information	Remarks and references to Appendices
PERUWELZ	16/12/18		Inspection of Units. General routine	
do.	17/12/18		Inspection of Units. Notification received that Lieut. P. McGOUGH, V.O.i/c. 290 Bde. R.F.A. granted special leave to Ireland 25/11/18 to 9/12/18, is unable to return this sickness. A.D.V.S. I Corps notified and replacement asked for.	A/C
do.	18/12/18		Conference V.Os heard. Lieut. CAMPBELL RICHMOND, Senior NOTTING. Complies weekly return.	A/C
do.	19/12/18		Weekly returns submitted to A.D.V.S. I Corps as follows - Horses. In last return 50. Admits 40. Total 90. Cures 31. Evacuees 3. Destroyed 1. Remaining 55. Total 90. Found. Strength 2390. Mostages nil. Mules. In last return 20. Admits 13. Total 33. Cures 10. Transfers 2. Destroyed 1. Remaining 20. Total 33. Strength 1202. Wastage 2.06%. General routine inspection of Units.	A/C
do.	20/12/18		General routine	A/C
do.	21/12/18		Lieut. DUNPHY, J.P. V.O.i/c. 26th A.F.A. Bde. report back from leave.	A/C
do.	22/12/18		Major J. SCOTT BOWDEN D.A.D.V.S. evacuated to hospital A.D.V.S. I Corps notified. Capt. J. CAMPBELL O.C. 58 Div. M.V.S. takes over duties as A/D.A.D.V.S.	A/C
do.	23/12/18		General routine	A/C

J. Campbell Capt.
A/D.A.D.V.S. 58 Divn.

Army Form C. 2118.

WAR DIARY
or
INTELLIGENCE SUMMARY.
(Erase heading not required.)

Instructions regarding War Diaries and Intelligence Summaries are contained in F.S. Regs., Part II. and the Staff Manual respectively. Title pages will be prepared in manuscript.

D.A.D.V.S.
56th DIVISION

(126)

Place	Date	Hour	Summary of Events and Information	Remarks and references to Appendices
BERUNEZ.	24/12/18		Office routine.	A/R
do.	25/12/18		do.	A/R
do.	26/12/18		Conference of A.D.S. present. Lieuts CAMPBELL, RICHMOND, Lieut McDONNOUGH. NOTTING. D.C. also Capt. DUNPHY. VO/c 267 Bde. A.F.A.	
do.	27/12/18		Weekly returns submitted to A.D.V.S. 1 Corps as follows:— Horses. In last return 55. Admitted 40. Total 191. Cured 21. Evacuated to Dit 1. Destroyed 1. Remaining 42. Total 191. Sick 1. Strength 2339. Wastage 1.5% Mules. In last return 20. Admitted 9. Total 29. Cured 5. Evacuated 3. Destroyed 2. Total 19. Total Bg. Strength 199. Wastage 3.4%	D S.S. A.R.
do.	28/12/18		Inspection of Amb. Muck. + Office routine.	D.D. S.S.
do.	29/12/18		- do -	A.R.
do.	30/12/18		- do -	
do.	31/12/18		Lieut. J.L. MILLER R.A.V.C. reports for duty, vice Lieut. P. McLAUGHLIN R.A.V.C. A/E and is posted to 290 Bde. R.F.A.	
			Date of Embarkation 19-1-19.	

J Campbell Ryan
A.D.V.S. 56 Div.

D. D. & L., London, E.C.
(A10260) Wt.W5900/P773 750,000 2/18 Sch. 52 Forms/C2118/16

WAR DIARY
or
INTELLIGENCE SUMMARY

Army Form C. 2118.

D.A.D.V.S. 58th Division
No. 3/1/19

Place	Date	Hour	Summary of Events and Information	Remarks and references to Appendices
PERUWELZ	Jan 1st/1919		General Routine.	1/1/19 RLH
do.	2/1/19		Conference of V.O.S. Present Capts CAMPBELL, RICHMOND, DUNPHY. Lieuts NOTTING & MILLER.	RLH
do	3/1/19		Weekly returns submitted to H.D.V.S. 1 Corps as follows:- HORSES. Indent return 142 Admitted 36 Total 178 Cured transfers etc. to Depôt mge. 1. Remaining under treatment 45. Dead 78 Mules Indent return 19 Admitted 4 RLH. Total 23 Cured 28 Transfers etc 4 Destroyed 2 Remaining 19. Total 28 Strength Horses 2324 Mules Mnge 72k. Mules Sturgt 1194 Mnture 53k.	RLH
do	4/1/19		Sale of army Horses and Mules to Civilians at PERUWELZ.	RLH
do	5/1/19		Major R.L.L. HART. R.A.V.C. arrived to assume duties as D.A.D.V.S. All concerned notified.	RLH
do	6/1/19		General office routine. Inspection of M.V.S. shipping Classification of animals in R. Division.	RLH
do	7/1/19		Classification of animals in D.T.M.B. Units & Signal Coy.	RLH
do	8/1/19		Inspection & Classification of animals in 24, 22, 23 Inf. Bn. F.T.	RLH
do	9/1/19		Visits A.D.V.S. 1 Corps. Conference V.O. Officers present Capts RICHMOND, CAMPBELL, DUNPHY Lieuts NOTTING, MILLER. Compiling weekly returns.	RLH

WAR DIARY
INTELLIGENCE SUMMARY

Army Form C. 2118.

D.A.D.V.S. 58TH DIVISION

Place	Date	Hour	Summary of Events and Information	Remarks and references to Appendices
PERUWELZ	10/11/1918		Divisional Veterinary Board, composed of Major R.L. HART D.A.D.V.S, Capt CAMPBELL D.D.S. Div. V.S. & Capt RICHMOND, inspected and classified animals of 174 Infantry Bde. Weekly returns submitted to A.D.V.S. 1 Corps as follows:-	
	11/11/1918		HORSES. In last returns 45. Admitted 41. Total 86. Cured 22. Evacuated. Sick 17. Died 1. Remaining understrength to Total 86. Strength 2310. Wastage 1.8%. Mules - In last return 10 evacuated. Remaining 11 Total 32.	
do	12/11/1918		Inoc 32 Cured 13 transferred 4 destroyed 1 Remaining in reg. 13. Strength 1/143. Wastage 42%.	
do	13/11/1918		Classification of animals in 173 Infantry Bde.	
do	14/11/1918		Classification of animals in M.T.S.	
do	15/11/1918		Classification of animals in 175 Infantry Bde.	
			do do 290 Bde R.F.A.	
			do do 291 -	
			do do 58 D.A.C.	
do	16/11/1918		To A.D.V.S. 1 Corps showing 2053 for evacuation from Civil Divisions. For the date 17 Oxford.	

Army Form C. 2118.

WAR DIARY
or
INTELLIGENCE SUMMARY.
(Erase heading not required.)

Instructions regarding War Diaries and Intelligence Summaries are contained in F. S. Regs., Part II. and the Staff Manual respectively. Title pages will be prepared in manuscript.

D.A.D.V.S.
58TH DIVISION
No. 3/1/19.
Date.

Place	Date	Hour	Summary of Events and Information	Remarks and references to Appendices
PERUWELZ	17/1/19.		Veterinary Classification of animals in 26th Army Bn. A.E.F.	R.M.H.
do	18/1/19.		Sale of Army horses and Mules to Civilians at PERUWELZ. Weekly return submitted to A.D.V.S. Loads as follows: Horses. On hand return to Army 18. Total on Estab: 21. Destroyed 1. Remaining unrepresent N3. Total on Strength 22½. Mules In last return admitted in Total 23. Ewes 3. Remaining on Estab 23. Mules 10 kill.	R.M.H.
do	19/1/19.		General Routine.	R.M.H.
do	20/1/19.		Inspection and Classification of 509 + 510 Coys R.A.S.C. or Suffolks	R.M.H.
do	21/1/19.		Classification of animals in M.G. Bn and Field Coy R.E.	R.M.H.
do	22/1/19.		Malleining animals in Div Coy. Inspected class 'J' animals at PERUWELZ.	R.M.H.
do	23/1/19.		Classification of animals 57 Coy. R.A.S.C. Malleining animals 2/3 No. F.A. Issued Dg Cy tractors.	R.M.H.
do	24/1/19.		Inspection of No F.A. animals in Malleinment.	R.M.H.

Army Form C. 2118.

WAR DIARY
or
INTELLIGENCE-SUMMARY.
(Erase heading not required.)

D.A.D.V.S.,
58TH DIVISION
No... 31/1/19

Instructions regarding War Diaries and Intelligence Summaries are contained in F.S. Regs., Part II. and the Staff Manual respectively. Title pages will be prepared in manuscript.

Place	Date	Hour	Summary of Events and Information	Remarks and references to Appendices
PERUWELZ	24/1/19		Weekly returns submitted to A.D.V.S. I Corps. as follows:- Horses. In last return 42. Admitted since 39. Total 79. Cured 17. Transferred 10. Died 1. Destroyed 7. Remaining at Total 79. Strength 2183. Wastage .74 %. Mules. In last return 18 admits 1. Total 35. Cured 11. Transferred 3. Died 1. Remaining 20. Total 35. Strength 1223. Wastage .23 %. General. Bon fire & Officer Canteen.	MW
do	25/1/19		do	LMW, GMW, 40W, FMW
do	26/1/19		do	WW
do	27/1/19		Mallening H.Q. R.A. animals & 2/1 H.C. F.A.	
do	28/1/19		Inspecting animals for Meeken ranch	
do	29/1/19		Wire despatched to A.D.V.S. I Corps giving numbers of animals & vehicles to date as follows:- Horses. Class A. 403. B. 1084 & 116 & 1503 D.20. Total 2664. Mules. Class A. 412. B. 539. C. 401. D. 7. Total 1412. Conference 11 a.m. of all M.S. Piesel, Carr & Campbell Richmond, Dunphy, Reus, Notting & Miller. Mallening D.H.Q. Horses Sig Coy M.M.?	WW
do	30/1/19		Mallening S.H.Q. M.M.P. Horses at the WM.P. Three months comparative weekly return.	WW

Army Form C. 2118.

WAR DIARY
or
INTELLIGENCE SUMMARY
(Erase heading not required.)

Instructions regarding War Diaries and Intelligence Summaries are contained in F.S. Regs., Part II. and the Staff Manual respectively. Title pages will be prepared in manuscript.

D.A.D.V.S.
58TH DIVISION.
No. 31/1/9

Place	Date	Hour	Summary of Events and Information	Remarks and references to Appendices
PERONNE	31/1/19		150 Class of Horses Handed to Base for shipment to U.K. T.O.360. Capt ATTENBOROUGH. P.G. R.A.V.C. Attached 173 Inf. Bde. Despatched for demobilization. Weekly returns submitted:- A.D.V.S. 1 Corps as follows:- Horses. In last return in admitted 18. Total 63 Curer in Dies 1. Destroyed 2. Remaining 44. Total 62. Destroyed 1 Dehorsed 2. Remaining 44. Total 62. Strength 2191 Mokes 14% Mules. In last return 20. admitted 5. Total 25. Cures 7. Remaining 18. Total 25. Strength 1230 Working Mls.	R/H
			Date of embarkation 19-1-1919	

Ralph P. Hart
Major,
D.A.D.V.S.
58th (LONDON) DIVISION.

www.ingramcontent.com/pod-product-compliance
Lightning Source LLC
Chambersburg PA
CBHW081424160426
43193CB00013B/2186